Jump Into Math

Strategies to Help Students Succeed with Computation

Grade 5

by
Barry Doran, EdS
Leland Graham, PhD

D1716746

Carson-Dellosa Publishing Company, Inc.
Greensboro, North Carolina

 This book has been correlated to state, national, and Canadian provincial standards.
Visit *www.carsondellosa.com* to search for and view its correlations to your standards.

Editors: Carrie Fox and Beki Benning

Layout Design: Lori Jackson

Inside Illustrations: Jenny Campbell

Cover Design: Lori Jackson and Peggy Jackson

ISBN: 978-1-60022-096-8

Table of Contents

Skills Index

CD-104227 • Jump Into Math • © Carson-Dellosa

Skills Index

Introducing *Jump Into Math*
• A DIAGNOSTIC GUIDE •

Jump Into Math is designed to provide practical suggestions for overcoming common stumbling blocks students encounter with computational skills. Often, teachers have difficulty planning a meaningful and successful corrective instructional program for learners who are having trouble with computational skills. *Jump Into Math* is a ready-to-use program of study for these struggling learners that offers a systematic analysis of troublesome concepts, step-by-step instruction for teachers, and meaningful practice for students.

Overview

The development of computational skills is a major component of any mathematics program. Computation is included in the Numbers and Operations strand as outlined by The National Council of Teachers of Mathematics in their *Principles and Standards for School Mathematics* (2000). The NCTM Standards advocate computational fluency for students and further suggest that students who are able to compute efficiently and accurately can significantly increase their scores on standardized tests and build a sturdy foundation for success with higher math, such as algebra. Poor computation skills are a significant handicap to many mathematics students. Therefore, a comprehensive diagnosis of students' errors and misconceptions in arithmetic, followed by corrective instruction and focused practice, is essential.

Computational errors are not always the result of carelessness or improper procedures. Teachers sometimes have the misconception that "practice makes perfect," but perfection comes with improvement over time. If students practice the same mistakes over and over again, improvement will be slow or will not happen at all. For a student to improve and reach "perfection," the "practice" must be accompanied by carefully planned developmental instruction that is designed to help students overcome their specific problems.

Careful observations of students at work and an analysis of their written work are key components of meaningful instruction. There are four general categories of errors in computation: wrong operation, fact errors, defective algorithms, and random responses (guessing). Most student errors can be eliminated if they have a thorough understanding of the procedures used to perform a computation. This requires the student to experience hands-on practice with the underlying skills and concepts. Teachers must plan a developmental sequence of skills that provides the struggling learner with success-oriented experiences that eliminate frustration and failure.

How to Use *Jump Into Math*

Each grade-level book in the *Jump Into Math* series is divided into specific number and computational skills. Each section includes a diagnostic test with teacher notes, teaching activities, and student activities targeted to specific items on the test. In addition, a comprehensive test is included at the end of the book. The components of the *Jump Into Math* program are described below.

Diagnostic Tests—The diagnostic tests target the fundamental concepts of each skill. The tests are illustrative and can be modified by the teacher to meet individual program requirements. The intent is to provide an example of how diagnostic tests can be used to analyze students' errors. Some teachers will want to use the tests in order. Others may want to begin with Part II or Part III then, based on students' scores, either drop back to Part I or move on to other parts. The diagnostic tests may also be used to quickly determine placement of new students who enroll during the school year.

Teacher Notes and Teaching Activities—Following each diagnostic test is an analysis of each part of the test that references the specific skills addressed in each test item. The teacher notes have been designed to provide information about potential problem areas for students. Sample teaching strategies, activities, sample problems, and suggestions for follow-up instruction are included.

Student Activities—Student activities for practice are included for each problem type on the diagnostic tests. These activities provide practice of the skills, remediation, reteaching, extension to related skills, and maintenance of skills (review). Each practice page is correlated to a specific test item.

Comprehensive Test—At the end of the book, there is a multiple-choice test that includes items covering all of the computational skills appropriate to the grade level.

Diagnostic Test: Numeration

Directions: Write your answer to each question in the space provided.

Part I: Place Value to the Billions Period

1. What digit is in the billions place?

   2,387,654,190

   _____

2. What is the place value of the underlined digit?

   7,895,910,342

   _____

3. Write the name of the missing place value period.

   Billions

   Millions

   Ones

   _____

4. The underlined digits are in which period?

   1,903,427,586

   _____

5. Write the short word name for the number 1,032,398,705.

   1 _____

   32 _____

   398 _____

   705 _____

6. Write the number two billion forty-five million six hundred seventy-eight thousand nine hundred one.

   _____

7. What is the place value of the underlined digit?

    7̲1,946,803,270

    _____

8. What is the value of the underlined digit?

    514,9̲76,437,805

    _____

9. Write the number below in standard form.

    3,000,000,000 + 200,000,000 + 10,000,000 + 6,000,000 + 700,000 + 80,000 + 100 + 40 + 5

    _____

10. Write 3,071,542,896 in expanded form.

    _____

    _____

    _____

    _____

TEACHER ASSESSMENT AREA

Directions: Shade the boxes that correspond to correct test items.

Skill	Item Number			
Writing Numbers	1	2	3	4
	5	6	7	8
Expanded Notation	9	10		

TOTAL CORRECT: _____

Teacher Notes and Activities

TEACHER NOTES: Writing Numbers
(Diagnostic Test Part I: Test Items 1–8)

Today, students are frequently exposed to large numbers. Numbers in the billions can be found in many newspapers, magazines, and television programs. Introduce the billions period with place value charts as shown below.

BILLIONS			MILLIONS			THOUSANDS			ONES		
Hundreds	Tens	Ones	Hundreds	Tens	Ones	Hundreds	Tens	Ones	Hundreds	Tens	Ones
		5	1	4	3	6	7	8	2	9	0

The place value charts above show the number **5,143,678,290**. Commas separate the billions, millions, thousands, and ones periods.

- In expanded form, the number is: **5,000,000,000 + 100,000,000 + 40,000,000 + 3,000,000 + 600,000 + 70,000 + 8,000 + 200 + 90**.

- In words, the number is: **five billion one hundred forty-three million six hundred seventy-eight thousand two hundred ninety**.

- In short word form the number is: **5 billion 143 million 678 thousand 290**.

TEACHING ACTIVITY: "Research Billions" (Writing Numbers)

One billion is a difficult number for many students to comprehend. Ask students to search in newspapers, in magazines, and on the Internet to find examples of numbers in the billions. Students should write down the numbers and what the numbers represent. For example, "Scientists tell us that Earth is 4.6 billion years old." That means it is 4,600,000,000 years old. We can also say that Earth is 4,600 million years old.

BILLIONS			MILLIONS			THOUSANDS			ONES		
Hundreds	Tens	Ones	Hundreds	Tens	Ones	Hundreds	Tens	Ones	Hundreds	Tens	Ones
		4	6	0	0	0	0	0	0	0	0

Divide a chalkboard into the billions period, millions period, thousands period, and ones period as shown above. Choose students to be the billions recorder, millions recorder, thousands recorder, and ones recorder. As students read and describe their numbers, the recorders should write the numbers in the chart. Continue until there are 10 numbers on the chalkboard.

Practice reading each number aloud. Ask students questions such as, "Which number is the largest? Smallest?" Help students order the numbers and write them in expanded form.

TEACHER NOTES: Expanded Notation

(Diagnostic Test Part I: Test Items 9–10)

Students must be able to write large numbers in expanded form, standard form, word form, and short word form. Encourage students to use place value charts as references while they practice writing large numbers in different forms.

TEACHING ACTIVITIES: "Patterns" (Expanded Notation)

Help students understand the relationships between large numbers by using patterns like the ones shown below.

- 1 hundred thousand = **100 x 1,000 (a hundred thousands)**
- 1 million = **1,000 x 1,000 (a thousand thousands)**
- 1 billion = **1,000 x 1,000,000 (a thousand millions)**

"Expanded Form and Word Forms" (Expanded Notation)

Discuss the following ways to write large numbers with your students. For example, there are several different ways to write 4,600,000,000:

- Expanded Form: **4,000,000,000 + 600,000,000**
- Word Form: **Four billion six hundred million**
- Short Word Form: **4.6 billion**

NAME: _____   DATE: _____

What's My Place?

Writing Numbers

Test Items 1–8

Directions: Write the digit in each place named.

Write the digit in the **thousands** place.

1. 218,255,586 _____   2. 78,359,986 _____

3. 561,826,736 _____   4. 855,360,456 _____

Write the digit in the **ten millions** place.

5. 143,678,290 _____   6. 938,579,468 _____

7. 259,456,098 _____   8. 36,456,987 _____

9. 581,543,632 _____

Write the digit in the **billions** place.

10. 3,463,856,157 _____   11. 9,357,951,369 _____

12. 6,358,569,321 _____   13. 5,582,357,405 _____

14. 7,321,782,103 _____

What's My Value?

Directions: Write the place value of the underlined digit. Then, give the digit's value.

1. 21,6<u>3</u>5,879

    _____

    _____

2. 5<u>4</u>,637,258

    _____

    _____

3. <u>3</u>17,357,456

    _____

    _____

4. 45<u>6</u>,147,256

    _____

    _____

5. 1<u>7</u>,597,181

    _____

    _____

6. <u>8</u>50,265,105

    _____

    _____

7. <u>7</u>1,946,803,270

    _____

    _____

8. 51<u>4</u>,976,437,805

    _____

    _____

Reading and Writing Numbers

Expanded Notation

Test Items 9–10

Directions: Write each number's word form, short word form, and expanded form.

1. **7,151,741**

   Word Form: _____

   _____

   Short Word Form: _____

   Expanded Form: _____

   _____

2. **23,432,231**

   Word Form: _____

   _____

   Short Word Form: _____

   Expanded Form: _____

   _____

3. **50,263,109**

   Word Form: _____

   _____

   Short Word Form: _____

   Expanded Form: _____

   _____

4. **7,780,500,545**

   Word Form: _____

   _____

   Short Word Form: _____

   Expanded Form: _____

   _____

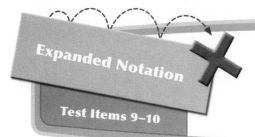

Mixed Practice

Directions: Circle the letter beside each correct answer.

1. **8,560,420** written in word form is:
   A. eight million five hundred sixty thousand four hundred
   B. eight million five hundred sixty thousand four hundred twenty
   C. eight hundred thousand five hundred sixty four hundred twenty
   D. eight million sixty thousand four hundred twenty

2. The standard form of **400,000 + 80,000 + 5,000 + 600 + 70 + 8** is:
   A. 408,568   B. 485,678   C. 48,567   D. 485,670

3. **58,060,562** in expanded form is:
   A. 50,000,000 + 8,000,000 + 60,000 + 500 + 60 + 2
   B. 50,000,000 + 80,000,000 + 600,000 + 500 + 60 + 2
   C. 5,000,000 + 8,000,000 + 6,000,000 + 500 + 60 + 2
   D. 58,000,000 + 60,000 + 5,000 + 60 + 20

4. What is **six billion five hundred eighty million four hundred thousand three hundred forty-five** in standard form?
   A. 65,080,400,345   C. 6,580,445
   B. 6,500,400,345   D. 6,580,400,345

5. The standard form for **20,000,000 + 9,000,000 + 50,000 + 3,000 + 300 + 30 + 3** is:
   A. 2,675,333   B. 29,053,333   C. 20,953,033   D. 29,530,333

6. **40,500,300,291** in word form is:
   A. forty million five hundred thousand two hundred ninety-one
   B. forty-five billion three hundred thousand two hundred ninety-one
   C. forty billion five hundred million three hundred thousand two hundred ninety-one
   D. forty billion five hundred thirty million three hundred thousand two hundred ninety-one

7. The standard form of **3,000,000 + 500,000 + 60,000 + 4,000 + 500 + 70 + 5** is:
   A. 35,604,575   C. 3,560,575
   B. 3,564,575   D. 3,560,075

Diagnostic Test: Numeration

Directions: Write your answer to each question in the space provided.

Part II: Decimal Place Value

1. What is the place value of the underlined digit?

    356.2$\underline{4}$7

    _____

2. Write the following number in standard form.

    $3 + \dfrac{3}{10} + \dfrac{5}{100} + \dfrac{8}{1000}$

    _____

3. Write the number **two hundred thirty-four and fifty-seven hundredths** in standard form.

    _____

4. What is the place value of the underlined digit?

    234.$\underline{8}$39

    _____

5. Write the following number in standard form.

    $300 + 10 + 5 + \dfrac{3}{10} + \dfrac{5}{100}$

    _____

6. Write **17.328** in expanded fractional form.

    _____

7. Use **<**, **>**, or **=** to compare the decimals.

    0.681 $\bigcirc$ 0.6809

8. Use **<**, **>**, or **=** to compare the decimals.

    0.622 $\bigcirc$ 0.637

9. Write the decimals in order from greatest to least.

    0.45

    0.54

    0.05

    0.04

    _____

    _____

    _____

    _____

10. Write the decimals in order from greatest to least.

    4.56

    6.54

    4.44

    5.56

    4.65

    _____

    _____

    _____

    _____

    _____

TEACHER ASSESSMENT AREA

Directions: Shade the boxes that correspond to correct test items.

Skill	Item Number			
Place Value to the Thousandths Place	1	2	3	4
	5	6		
Comparing and Ordering Decimals	7	8	9	10

TOTAL CORRECT: _____

Teacher Notes and Activities

TEACHER NOTES: Place Value to the Thousandths Place
(Diagnostic Test Part II: Test Items 1–6)

Students have already been introduced to whole number place value as well as the concepts of fractions and decimals. Decimal place value should now be introduced. Begin by explaining how whole numbers are placed to the left of the decimal point and fractional numbers, or numbers that are less than 1, are placed to the right of the decimal point.

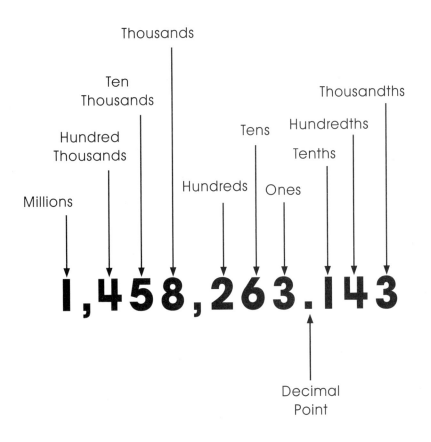

Ask students to look for a pattern in the names of the decimal place values. Students should observe how decimal and whole number place value names are alike and how they are different. Ask students to predict what other decimal place values are named based on observed patterns. Teach students to read decimals according to the place value of the last digits. In the example above, the decimal portion of the number (.143) ends in the thousandths place. So the decimal is read, "one hundred forty-three thousandths."

TEACHING ACTIVITY: "Reading and Writing Decimals"
(Place Value to the Thousandths Place)

Introduce the place value chart below to students. Explain that the digits to the left of the decimal are whole numbers and the digits to the right of the decimal are fractional numbers.

Then, focus on the place values to the right of the decimal point. Use the place value chart to illustrate place value from ones to thousandths.

The place value chart shows the number 3.143, which is read, "three and one hundred forty-three thousandths." Point out to students that the decimal is read as "and."

The place value chart can also remind students of how to write decimal numbers in expanded form. In the example above, the expanded form is written as $3 + \frac{1}{10} + \frac{4}{100} + \frac{3}{1000}$.

Students should practice writing each number presented in the place value chart in standard form, expanded form, and word form.

PLACE VALUE CHART				
Ones	Decimal Point	Tenths	Hundredths	Thousandths
I	.	$\frac{1}{10}$	$\frac{1}{100}$	$\frac{1}{1000}$
1.0		0.1	0.01	0.001
3	**.**	**1**	**4**	**3**
1. 3	.	1		
2. 5	.	3	2	
3. 0	.	2	8	
4. 8	.	0	4	5
5. 4	.	2	6	8

TEACHER NOTES: Comparing and Ordering Decimals

(Diagnostic Test Part II: Test Items 7–10)

Comparing and ordering numbers is dependent upon place value, whether working with whole numbers or decimals. Review comparing and ordering whole numbers with students, reminding them that they will use the same place value method to compare and order decimals.

TEACHING ACTIVITIES

"Reviewing Whole Numbers" (Comparing and Ordering Decimals)

Review by demonstrating the following problem on a chalkboard for students.

Which is greater, 567 or 565?

H	T	O
5	6	7
5	6	5

To compare 567 and 565, line the numbers up by place value as shown above.

Look for the first place value where the numbers are different, starting at the left. The hundreds places are both 5, and the tens places are both 6. The first difference is between the 7 and the 5 in the ones place. So, 567 > 565 because 7 > 5.

"Comparing Decimals" (Comparing and Ordering Decimals)

To compare decimals, the place value method can be used as with whole numbers. The digits must be lined up, using the decimal point as a reference. Demonstrate the following problem on a chalkboard for students.

Which is greater, 5.67 or 5.654?

O		T	H	TH
5	.	6	7	
5	.	6	5	4

The ones and the tenths places both match. The first difference is in the hundredths place, where 7 > 5. So, 5.67 > 5.654.

Students should practice comparing decimals with the following problems. Use >, <, or = to compare.

1. 1.4 ◯ 1.39   2. 20.107 ◯ 20.196   3. 0.565 ◯ 0.510   4. 8.01 ◯ 8.001

"Ordering Decimals" (Comparing and Ordering Decimals)

The procedure used for comparing decimals can be used to order decimals as well. Remind students to line up numbers by decimal points. Review the examples below with students.

Order 0.68, 0.08, 0.32, and 0.01 from greatest to least.
Rewrite the numbers vertically, lining up the decimal points.

O		T	H
0	.	6	8
0	.	0	8
0	.	3	2
0	.	0	1

The digits in the ones place are all the same. Compare the digits in the tenths place. Order the numbers from greatest to least: 6 > 3, so 0.68 > 0.32.

Because 0.08 and 0.01 each have a 0 in the tenths place, compare the digits in the hundredths place. Order the numbers from greatest to least: 8 > 1, so 0.08 > 0.01.

0.68, 0.32, 0.08, 0.01

Order 4.56, 6.54, 4.44, 5.56, and 4.65 from greatest to least.
Rewrite the numbers vertically, lining up the decimal points.

O		T	H
4	.	5	6
6	.	5	4
4	.	4	4
5	.	5	6
4	.	6	5

Begin by comparing the digits in the ones place: 6 > 5, so 6.54 > 5.56.

Because the remaining numbers all have a 4 in the ones place, compare the digits in the tenths place. Order from greatest to least: 6 > 5 > 4, so 4.65 > 4.56 > 4.44.

6.54, 5.56, 4.65, 4.56, 4.44

Students should practice ordering numbers with the following sets. Ask students to order the decimals from greatest to least.

1. 1.23, 2.43, 1.09, 2.23, 2.63

2. 0.098, 0.867, 0.126, 0.011, 0.345

Understanding Decimals

Directions: Study the place value diagram below. Then, answer the following questions. Remember that digits to the **left of the decimal** are whole numbers and digits to the **right of the decimal** are fractional numbers.

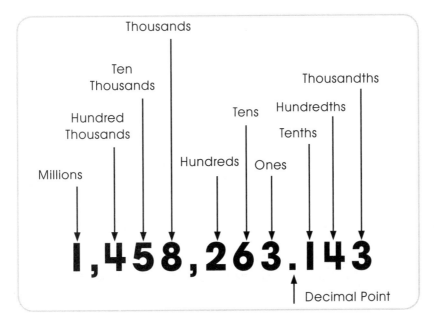

1. What is the place value of the underlined digit?

    345.9<u>8</u>

    _____

2. What is the place value of the underlined digit?

    234.3<u>8</u>9

    _____

3. What is the place value of the underlined digit?

    564.23<u>6</u>

    _____

4. What is the place value of the underlined digit?

    867.<u>6</u>3

    _____

5. What is the place value of the underlined digit?

    673.94<u>2</u>

    _____

6. What is the place value of the underlined digit?

    940.<u>0</u>38

    _____

NAME: _____ DATE: _____

Decimals in Many Forms

Directions: Study the place value chart below. Then, answer the following questions.

PLACE VALUE CHART				
Ones	Decimal Point	Tenths	Hundredths	Thousandths
I		$\frac{1}{10}$	$\frac{1}{100}$	$\frac{1}{1000}$
1.0	.	0.1	0.01	0.001
3	**.**	**1**	**4**	**3**

The place value chart shows the number **3.143**.

Word form: **three and one hundred forty-three thousandths**

Expanded form: $3 + \frac{1}{10} + \frac{4}{100} + \frac{3}{1000}$

1. Write $3 + \frac{3}{10} + \frac{5}{100} + \frac{8}{1000}$ in standard form: _____

2. Write the number **six and seven hundred eighty-one thousandths**: _____

3. Write $300 + 10 + 5 + \frac{1}{10} + \frac{2}{100}$ in standard form: _____

4. Write the number **nine and seven hundred sixty-eight thousandths**: _____

5. Write 17.328 in expanded form: _____

6. Write the number **four and five hundred ten thousandths**: _____

7. Write the number **twenty-nine and five thousandths**: _____

Charting Decimals

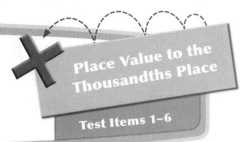

Place Value to the
Thousandths Place

Test Items 1–6

Directions: Look at the example in the chart below. Then, complete the rest of the chart by writing the expanded form and word form of each number given.

STANDARD FORM	EXPANDED FORM	WORD FORM
1. 2.1	$2 + \dfrac{1}{10}$	two and one tenth
2. 5.32		
3. 0.28		
4. 8.045		
5. 3.47		
6. 1.15		
7. 2.503		
8. 7.32		
9. 4.222		
10. 8.6		

Place Value to the
Thousandths Place

Test Items 1–6

Reading Decimals

Directions: Read each decimal in word form. Find the matching decimal in standard form below and write its letter beside the number word.

1. three hundred and five tenths _____

2. one and twelve thousandths _____

3. fifteen and sixty-seven hundredths _____

4. nine and nine thousandths _____

5. thirteen hundredths _____

6. nine and seven hundred sixty-eight thousandths _____

7. four and two hundred twenty-five thousandths _____

8. three and seven tenths _____

9. forty-five and sixteen hundredths _____

A. 9.768	B. 15.67	C. 45.16	D. 9.009	E. 4.225

F. 1.012	G. 0.13	H. 300.5	I. 3.7

NAME:_____ DATE:_____

Which Is Greater?

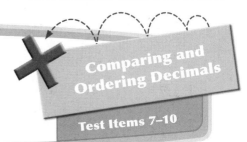

Comparing and
Ordering Decimals

Test Items 7–10

Directions: Study the example. Then, compare each pair of numbers below using **>**, **<**, or **=**.

Example: To compare decimals, line up the digits, using the decimal point as a reference. Compare **5.67** and **5.654**.

O		T	H	TH
5	.	6	7	
5	.	6	5	4

Compare digits, starting at the left.
The first difference is in the hundredths place, between 7 and 5.
Because 7 > 5, **5.67 > 5.654**.

1. 0.856 〇 0.862

2. 3.65 〇 36.5

3. 4.96 〇 5.02

4. 7.2 〇 7.162

5. 9.419 〇 8.42

6. 5.65 〇 56.5

7. 2.531 〇 25.31

8. 0.438 〇 0.43

9. 17.226 〇 17.326

10. 4.73 〇 4.073

11. 2.584 〇 2.584

12. 9.03 〇 9.03

13. 23.05 〇 2.305

14. 0.622 〇 0.637

15. 0.001 〇 0.010

Comparing Decimals

Directions: Use **>**, **<**, or **=** to compare the numbers below.

1. 1.4 ◯ 1.36   2. 0.565 ◯ 0.510   3. 8.01 ◯ 8.001

4. 0.87 ◯ 0.78   5. 45.21 ◯ 45.32   6. 0.951 ◯ 0.981

7. 53.274 ◯ 53.274   8. 85.61 ◯ 81.56   9. 9.541 ◯ 3.054

10. 12.79 ◯ 12.97   11. 20.107 ◯ 20.196   12. 12.84 ◯ 12.93

13. 15.14 ◯ 15.41   14. 0.281 ◯ 0.281   15. 258.4 ◯ 251.3

16. 32.54 ◯ 52.48   17. 27.18 ◯ 27.81   18. 96.03 ◯ 96.03

19. 54.43 ◯ 52.48   20. 39.42 ◯ 39.4   21. 32.23 ◯ 32.23

CD-104227 • Jump Into Math • © Carson-Dellosa

Decimals from Greatest to Least

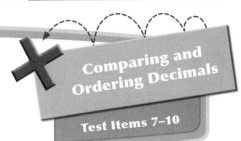

Comparing and Ordering Decimals

Test Items 7–10

Directions: Study the example. Then, order the decimals below from greatest to least.

To order decimals, you must first compare them. Line up the digits, using the decimal point as a reference. Order **0.68**, **0.08**, **0.32**, and **0.01** from greatest to least.

Compare the digits, starting at the left. The first difference is in the tenths place, so order the numbers with a digit in the tenths place from greatest to least. Because 6 > 3, 0.68 > 0.32.

O		T	H
0	.	6	8
0	.	0	8
0	.	3	2
0	.	0	1

Because 0.08 and 0.01 each have a 0 in the tenths place, compare the hundredths place and order from greatest to least. Because 8 > 1, 0.08 > 0.01. The correct order from greatest to least is: **0.68**, **0.32**, **0.08**, **0.01**.

1. 0.08   0.80   0.008

_____

2. 3.016   3.6   3.36

_____

3. 5.007   5.7   5.07

_____

4. 9.4   0.94   9.04

_____

5. 6.503   6.053   65.03

_____

6. 0.7   0.07   7.6   0.706

_____

7. 0.55   0.055   5.50   5.05

_____

8. 16.457   16.45   16.461   16.46

_____

9. 0.458   0.4508   0.4058   0.0458

_____

10. 6.4   0.064   64.04   0.604

_____

Correct Order?

Directions: If the numbers are ordered correctly from greatest to least, shade the list.

1.
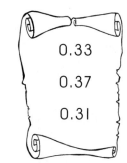
0.33
0.37
0.31

2.

19.20
19.17
19.15

3.
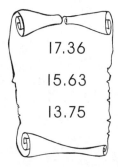
17.36
15.63
13.75

4.
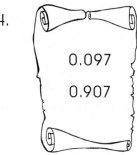
0.097
0.907

5.
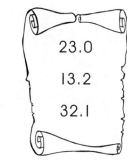
23.0
13.2
32.1

6.
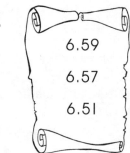
6.59
6.57
6.51

7.
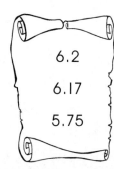
6.2
6.17
5.75

8.
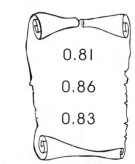
0.81
0.86
0.83

9.
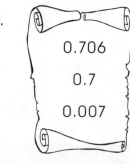
0.706
0.7
0.007

10.
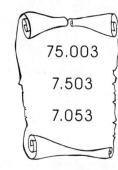
75.003
7.503
7.053

11.
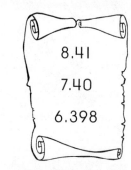
8.41
7.40
6.398

12.
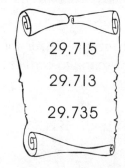
29.715
29.713
29.735

CD-104227 • Jump Into Math • © Carson-Dellosa

Diagnostic Test: Multiplication and Division Review

Directions: Write your answer to each question in the space provided. Show your work.

Part I: Multiplication

1.　　50
　　 x 6

2.　　400
　　 x　8

3.　　3,000
　　 x　　7

4.　　689
　　 x　5

5.　　2,437
　　 x　　6

6.　　58
　　 x 9

7.　　68
　　 x 43

8.　　49
　　 x 27

9.　　734
　　 x 29

10.　　482
　　 x 34

TEACHER ASSESSMENT AREA

Directions: Shade the boxes that correspond to correct test items.

Skill	Item Number		
Multiplying Tens, Hundreds, and Thousands	1	2	3
Multiplying Two to Four Digits by One Digit	4	5	6
Multiplying Two Digits by Two Digits	7	8	
Multiplying Three Digits by Two Digits	9	10	

TOTAL CORRECT:_____

Teacher Notes and Activities

TEACHER NOTES: Multiplication

(Diagnostic Test Part I: Test Items 1–10)

Some students will have difficulty with certain types of multiplication problems, even though this skill should be mastered by the end of fourth grade. The learning gap between those who have mastered multiplication and those who have not begins to widen in fifth grade. Intervention at this grade level needs to be diagnostic and prescriptive in order to lessen this gap. It is important to diagnose students' specific trouble areas to provide appropriate remediation. In this section, several types of multiplication problems are reviewed. Based on students' performance on the diagnostic test, provide them with specific practice for the problem types that were incorrect.

PROBLEM TYPES AND TEACHING EXAMPLES

PROBLEM TYPE	REMEDIATION	TEST ITEMS/WORKSHEETS
Multiplying Tens, Hundreds, and Thousands $\begin{array}{r} 30 \\ \times\ 6 \\ \hline \end{array}$ $\begin{array}{r} 200 \\ \times\ \ 7 \\ \hline \end{array}$ $\begin{array}{r} 4,000 \\ \times\ \ \ \ 8 \\ \hline \end{array}$	Review the basic multiplication facts. Demonstrate the pattern that develops when multiples of basic facts are multiplied. $3 \times 2 = 6$ $30 \times 2 = 60$ $300 \times 2 = 600$ $3,000 \times 2 = 6,000$ Teach students to use the short method: Multiply the basic fact. Count the number of zeros in the problem. Write that number of zeros to the right of the basic fact's product. $\begin{array}{r} 500 \\ \times\ \ \ 5 \\ \hline 2,500 \end{array}$ **Think:** $5 \times 5 = 25$. Write the 25. Count the zeros in the problem: 2 zeros. Write the zeros to the right of 25: 2,500.	Test Items: 1–3 Worksheet pages 33–35

PROBLEM TYPE	REMEDIATION	TEST ITEMS/ WORKSHEETS
Multiplying Two to Four Digits by One Digit 32 418 5,134 x 6 x 7 x 5	Use the partial product method until students have a clear understanding of the multiplication algorithm. 32 x 6 12 (6 x 2) +180 (6 x 30) 192 418 x 7 56 (7 x 8) 70 (7 x 10) +2,800 (7 x 400) 2,926 5,134 x 5 20 (5 x 4) 150 (5 x 30) 500 (5 x 100) + 25,000 (5 x 5,000) 25,670	Test Items: 4–6 Worksheet pages 36–38
Multiplying Two Digits by Two Digits 44 x 23	Multiplying a two-digit number by 11 or 12 is a natural transition to multiplying by larger two-digit numbers. Because most students can multiply by 1 and 10, introduce two-digit by two-digit problems with ones like those below. 23 x 11 23 (1 x 23) + 230 (10 x 23) 253 25 x 12 50 (2 x 25) + 250 (10 x 25) 300 When students become proficient with multiplying by 11 and 12, move on to problems with larger numbers. Continue to use the partial product method. When you feel that students are ready, introduce the standard algorithm as shown below. 44 x 23 132 + 880 ←zero for placeholder 1,012 **Step 1:** Multiply the ones in the second factor by the ones and tens in the first factor. Regroup if needed. **Step 2:** Multiply the tens in the second factor by the ones and tens in the first factor. Use 0 as a placeholder as shown above. Regroup if needed. **Step 3:** Add the products.	Test Items: 7, 8 Worksheet pages 39–41

PROBLEM TYPE	REMEDIATION	TEST ITEMS/ WORKSHEETS
Multiplying Three Digits by Two Digits $$\begin{array}{r} 436 \\ \times\ 26 \\ \hline \end{array}$$	Students must be proficient with multiplying three digits by two digits before attempting multiplication of larger numbers. Demonstrate with the partial product method first so that students can see the steps involved. $$\begin{array}{r} 436 \\ \times\ 26 \\ \hline 36\ (6 \times 6) \\ 180\ (6 \times 30) \\ 2{,}400\ (6 \times 400) \\ 120\ (20 \times 6) \\ 600\ (20 \times 30) \\ +\ 8{,}000\ (20 \times 400) \\ \hline 11{,}336 \end{array}$$ Now, demonstrate the same problem with the standard algorithm. **Step 1:** Multiply the first factor by the ones in the second factor. Regroup if needed. $$\begin{array}{r} 23 \\ 436 \\ \times\ 26 \\ \hline 2{,}616 \end{array}$$ **Step 2:** Multiply the first factor by the tens in the second factor. Regroup if needed. $$\begin{array}{r} 1 \\ 436 \\ \times\ 26 \\ \hline 2{,}616 \\ 8{,}720 \end{array}$$ **Step 3:** Add the products. $$\begin{array}{r} 436 \\ \times\ 26 \\ \hline 2{,}616 \\ +\ 8{,}720 \\ \hline 11{,}336 \end{array}$$	Test Items: 9–10 Worksheet pages 42–44

Multiplying by 10s

Multiplying Tens, Hundreds, and Thousands

Test Items 1–3

Directions: Study the example below. Then, solve the multiplication problems.

Short method: Multiply the basic fact. Count the number of zeros in the problem. Write that number of zeros to the right of the basic fact's product.	$\begin{array}{r} 50 \\ \times\ 5 \\ \hline 250 \end{array}$	**Think:** 5 x 5 = 25. Write the 25. Count the zeros in the problem: I zero. Write the zeros to the right of 25: **250**.

1. $\begin{array}{r} 20 \\ \times\ 4 \\ \hline \end{array}$

2. $\begin{array}{r} 30 \\ \times\ 4 \\ \hline \end{array}$

3. $\begin{array}{r} 40 \\ \times\ 4 \\ \hline \end{array}$

4. $\begin{array}{r} 50 \\ \times\ 4 \\ \hline \end{array}$

5. $\begin{array}{r} 20 \\ \times\ 5 \\ \hline \end{array}$

6. $\begin{array}{r} 30 \\ \times\ 5 \\ \hline \end{array}$

7. $\begin{array}{r} 40 \\ \times\ 5 \\ \hline \end{array}$

8. $\begin{array}{r} 50 \\ \times\ 5 \\ \hline \end{array}$

9. $\begin{array}{r} 30 \\ \times\ 6 \\ \hline \end{array}$

10. $\begin{array}{r} 40 \\ \times\ 6 \\ \hline \end{array}$

11. $\begin{array}{r} 50 \\ \times\ 6 \\ \hline \end{array}$

12. $\begin{array}{r} 60 \\ \times\ 6 \\ \hline \end{array}$

13. $\begin{array}{r} 40 \\ \times\ 7 \\ \hline \end{array}$

14. $\begin{array}{r} 50 \\ \times\ 7 \\ \hline \end{array}$

15. $\begin{array}{r} 60 \\ \times\ 7 \\ \hline \end{array}$

16. $\begin{array}{r} 70 \\ \times\ 7 \\ \hline \end{array}$

Multiplying by 100s

Directions: Study the example below. Then, solve the multiplication problems.

Remember: Multiply the basic fact. Count the number of zeros in the problem. Write that number of zeros to the right of the basic fact's product.

$$\begin{array}{r} 3\!\!\!/00 \\ \times\ 5 \\ \hline 1,500 \end{array}$$

1.   200
     x 3
	2. 300
	     x 4
		3. 400
		     x 5
			4. 500
			     x 4

5.   200
     x 5
	6. 300
	     x 5
		7. 400
		     x 6
			8. 500
			     x 5

9.   300
     x 6
	10. 400
	     x 7
		11. 500
		     x 7
			12. 600
			     x 6

13.   400
     x 8
	14. 500
	     x 8
		15. 600
		     x 8
			16. 700
			     x 8

Multiplying by 1,000s

Directions: Solve the following multiplication problems.

1.   2,000
    x   3
	2. 3,000
	    x 4
		3. 5,000
		    x 4
			4. 4,000
			    x 4

5.   3,000
    x   5
	6. 4,000
	    x 5
		7. 5,000
		    x 5
			8. 6,000
			    x 5

9.   4,000
    x   6
	10. 5,000
	    x 6
		11. 6,000
		    x 7
			12. 7,000
			    x 7

13.   5,000
    x   8
	14. 6,000
	    x 8
		15. 7,000
		    x 8
			16. 8,000
			    x 8

Multiplying Two Digits by One Digit

Directions: Study the example below. Then, use the partial product method to solve the multiplication problems.

Example:

$$
\begin{array}{r}
32 \\
\times\ \ 6 \\
\hline
12\ (6 \times 2) \\
+\ 180\ (6 \times 30) \\
\hline
192
\end{array}
$$

1. 45
    x 4

2. 35
    x 5

3. 44
    x 4

4. 54
    x 4

5. 28
    x 5

6. 39
    x 5

7. 47
    x 5

8. 55
    x 5

9. 36
    x 6

10. 45
    x 6

11. 58
    x 6

12. 63
    x 6

13. 46
    x 7

14. 55
    x 7

15. 63
    x 7

16. 75
    x 7

Multiplying Three Digits by One Digit

Multiplying Two to Four Digits by One Digit

Test Items 4–6

Directions: Study the example below. Then, use the partial product method to solve the multiplication problems.

Example:

$$
\begin{array}{r}
418 \\
\times \quad 7 \\
\hline
56 \quad (7 \times 8) \\
70 \quad (7 \times 10) \\
+\ 2,800 \quad (7 \times 400) \\
\hline
\mathbf{2,926}
\end{array}
$$

1. 256
    x 4

2. 445
    x 7

3. 412
    x 8

4. 657
    x 9

5. 437
    x 5

6. 372
    x 8

7. 689
    x 5

8. 753
    x 7

9. 323
    x 6

10. 554
    x 6

11. 573
    x 8

12. 588
    x 9

NAME: _____ DATE: _____

Multiplying Four Digits by One Digit

Directions: Study the example below. Then, use the partial product method to solve the multiplication problems.

Example:

$$
\begin{array}{r}
5,134 \\
\times \quad 5 \\
\hline
20 \ (5 \times 4) \\
150 \ (5 \times 30) \\
500 \ (5 \times 100) \\
+\ 25,000 \ (5 \times 5,000) \\
\hline
\mathbf{25,670}
\end{array}
$$

1. 2,435
   x   3

2. 3,245
   x   5

3. 1,474
   x   5

4. 4,326
   x   6

5. 1,952
   x   8

6. 5,357
   x   5

7. 4,153
   x   8

8. 5,249
   x   6

9. 8,176
   x   6

10. 6,589
    x   8

11. 7,383
    x   7

12. 6,154
    x   8

CD-104227 • Jump Into Math • © Carson-Dellosa

Multiplying by 11 and 12

Directions: Study the examples below. Then, use the partial product method to solve the multiplication problems.

Examples:

```
      23                        25
  x   11                    x   12
      23  (1 x 23)              50  (2 x 25)
  + 230  (10 x 23)          + 250  (10 x 25)
      253                       300
```

1. 35
    x 12

2. 29
    x 11

3. 24
    x 11

4. 35
    x 11

5. 55
    x 12

6. 41
    x 12

7. 27
    x 12

8. 53
    x 11

9. 49
    x 12

10. 49
    x 11

11. 62
    x 11

12. 72
    x 12

13. 28
    x 12

14. 74
    x 11

15. 50
    x 12

16. 83
    x 12

17. 36
    x 11

18. 75
    x 11

19. 54
    x 12

20. 55
    x 11

Multiplying
Two Digits by
Two Digits

Test Items 7–8

Multiplying Two Digits by Two Digits

Directions: Solve the multiplication problems.

1. 48 x 22	2. 39 x 26	3. 34 x 28	4. 45 x 34	5. 55 x 29
6. 61 x 33	7. 57 x 35	8. 63 x 45	9. 54 x 32	10. 56 x 35
11. 66 x 28	12. 59 x 33	13. 63 x 44	14. 61 x 49	15. 58 x 43
16. 64 x 29	17. 65 x 37	18. 67 x 46	19. 69 x 45	20. 68 x 56

CD-104227 • Jump Into Math • © Carson-Dellosa

Check It Out

Multiplying Two Digits by Two Digits

Test Items 7–8

Directions: Look at the solved multiplication problems. Shade each problem that has a correct product. Use the work area at the bottom of the page to check the answers.

1. 48
   x 43
   2,064

2. 65
   x 49
   3,285

3. 76
   x 35
   2,660

4. 43
   x 63
   2,719

5. 57
   x 64
   3,648

6. 75
   x 86
   5,742

7. 45
   x 77
   3,365

8. 66
   x 87
   5,742

9. 92
   x 78
   7,176

WORK AREA

Multiplying Three Digits by Two Digits

Directions: Study the example below. Then, solve the multiplication problems.

Step I: Multiply by the **ones**. Regroup if needed.	**Step 2:** Use 0 as a placeholder. Multiply by the **tens**. Regroup if needed.	**Step 3:** Add the products.
23 436 x 2**6** 2,616	I 2̶3̶ 436 x **26** 2,616 8,72**0**	I 2̶3̶ 436 x 26 2,616 + 8,720 11,336

1. 115
   x 43

2. 143
   x 12

3. 256
   x 44

4. 237
   x 32

5. 415
   x 55

6. 304
   x 39

7. 417
   x 56

8. 536
   x 26

9. 593
   x 45

10. 555
    x 48

11. 527
    x 52

12. 590
    x 65

Multiplying Three Digits by Two Digits Practice

Multiplying Three Digits by Two Digits

Test Items 9–10

Directions: Solve the multiplication problems.

1. 640 x 15	2. 658 x 23	3. 742 x 58	4. 676 x 27	5. 735 x 36
6. 763 x 65	7. 782 x 34	8. 791 x 49	9. 664 x 74	10. 742 x 68
11. 678 x 56	12. 792 x 56	13. 588 x 78	14. 820 x 76	15. 633 x 75
16. 418 x 76	17. 759 x 95	18. 653 x 84	19. 746 x 77	20. 827 x 73

Multiplying
Three Digits
by Two Digits

Test Items 9–10

Multiplication Match-Ups

Directions: Find the product for each problem in the box below. Then, write the letter beside the correct product on the line below each problem. Use another sheet of paper to work if necessary.

1. 333 x 33 _____	2. 444 x 25 _____	3. 748 x 47 _____	4. 888 x 68 _____	5. 788 x 55 _____
6. 898 x 64 _____	7. 996 x 38 _____	8. 949 x 72 _____	9. 749 x 59 _____	10. 857 x 34 _____
11. 765 x 72 _____	12. 853 x 49 _____	13. 918 x 88 _____	14. 978 x 66 _____	15. 569 x 54 _____

Products

A. 68,328	B. 29,138	C. 55,080	D. 10,989	E. 44,191
F. 11,100	G. 57,472	H. 64,548	I. 30,726	J. 43,340
K. 35,156	L. 37,848	M. 41,797	N. 60,384	O. 80,784

CD-104227 • Jump Into Math • © Carson-Dellosa

Diagnostic Test:
Multiplication and Division Review

Directions: Write your answer to each question in the space provided.

Multiplication and Division Review Part II: Division

1. 4)‾31‾

2. 3)‾89‾

3. 5)‾793‾

4. 4)‾3,110‾

5. 6)‾47,286‾

6. 40)‾9,134‾

7. 20)‾672‾

8. 26)‾7,915‾

9. 39)‾17,948‾

10. 17)‾23,716‾

TEACHER ASSESSMENT AREA

Directions: Shade the boxes that correspond to correct test items.

TOTAL CORRECT:_____

Skill	Item Number		
Dividing Two Digits by One Digit	1	2	
Dividing Three to Five Digits by One Digit	3	4	5
Dividing by Multiples of 10	6	7	
Dividing by Two-Digit Divisors	8	9	10

Teacher Notes and Activities

TEACHER NOTES: Division
(Diagnostic Test Part I: Test Items 1–10)

Division is one of the most difficult whole-number operations for students to master, as well as one of the most difficult for teachers to teach. To master division, students must be able to correctly use multiplication, subtraction, and addition. The relationship between subtraction and division as well as multiplication and division must be fully understood if students are to divide correctly. Division skills are developed over several grade levels, and care must be exercised to ensure that consistent strategies are used.

PROBLEM TYPES AND TEACHING EXAMPLES

PROBLEM TYPE	REMEDIATION	TEST ITEMS/WORKSHEETS
Dividing Two Digits by One Digit $4\overline{)31}$ $3\overline{)89}$	The example below shows a two-digit number divided by a one-digit number, with the quotient written over the ones place. This indicates that the quotient is less than 10. $\begin{array}{r} 7\,\text{R}\,3 \\ 4\overline{)31} \\ -28 \\ \hline 3 \end{array}$ The example below shows a two-digit number divided by a one-digit number, with the first digit of the quotient written over the tens place. This indicates that the quotient is more than 9 and less than 100. $\begin{array}{r} 29\,\text{R}\,2 \\ 3\overline{)89} \\ -60 \\ \hline 29 \\ -27 \\ \hline 2 \end{array}$ Students may answer incorrectly in one or both types of two-digit by one-digit division. Check students' diagnostic test results to see which type was missed and provide specific practice.	Test Items 1–2 Worksheet pages 51–53

PROBLEM TYPE	REMEDIATION	TEST ITEMS/WORKSHEETS
Dividing Three to Five Digits by One Digit $5\overline{)118}$ $2\overline{)4{,}293}$ $5\overline{)12{,}351}$	Use place value charts to help students solve each problem in steps. Review the steps of the division algorithm. **THREE-DIGIT BY ONE-DIGIT DIVISION** **Step 1:** Divide the hundreds. **Step 2:** Divide the tens. **Step 3:** Divide the ones. **Step 4:** Find the remainder. **Place Value** **Standard Algorithm** $$\begin{array}{r} 23\text{ R }3 \\ 5\overline{)118} \\ -100 \\ \hline 18 \\ -15 \\ \hline 3 \end{array} \qquad \begin{array}{r} 23\text{ R }3 \\ 5\overline{)118} \\ -10\downarrow \\ \hline 18 \\ -15 \\ \hline 3 \end{array}$$ **FOUR-DIGIT BY ONE-DIGIT DIVISION** **Step 1:** Divide the thousands. **Step 2:** Divide the hundreds. **Step 3:** Divide the tens. **Step 4:** Divide the ones. **Step 5:** Find the remainder. **Place Value** **Standard Algorithm** $$\begin{array}{r} 2{,}146\text{ R }1 \\ 2\overline{)4{,}293} \\ -4{,}000 \\ \hline 293 \\ -200 \\ \hline 93 \\ -80 \\ \hline 13 \\ -12 \\ \hline 1 \end{array} \qquad \begin{array}{r} 2{,}146\text{ R }1 \\ 2\overline{)4{,}293} \\ -4\downarrow\downarrow\downarrow \\ \hline 0\,2 \\ -2\downarrow \\ \hline 09 \\ -8\downarrow \\ \hline 13 \\ -12 \\ \hline 1 \end{array}$$	Test Items: 3–5 Worksheet pages 54–56

PROBLEM TYPE	REMEDIATION	TEST ITEMS/WORKSHEETS
Dividing Three to Five Digits by One Digit (continued)	**FIVE-DIGIT BY ONE-DIGIT DIVISION** **Step 1:** Divide the ten thousands. **Step 2:** Divide the thousands. **Step 3:** Divide the hundreds. **Step 4:** Divide the tens. **Step 5:** Divide the ones. **Step 6:** Find the remainder. **Place Value** **Standard Algorithm** $$5)\overline{12{,}351} = 2{,}470\ R\ 1$$ $-10{,}000$ $\quad 2{,}351$ $-2{,}000$ $\quad\ \ 351$ $\ \ -350$ $\qquad\ \ 1$ $\qquad -0$ $\qquad\ \ 1$ Standard Algorithm: $2{,}470\ R\ 1$ $5)\overline{12{,}351}$ -10 $\ \ 23$ -20 $\ \ \ 35$ $\ -35$ $\quad\ 01$ $\quad -0$ $\qquad 1$	Test Items: 3–5 Worksheet pages 54–56
Divide by Multiples of 10 $20)\overline{670}$	Division by multiples of 10 is essential for development of the division by two-digit divisors skill. It also helps form an understanding of the relationship between multiplication and division. In the example below, instruct students to think of the problem as $2\text{ tens})\overline{\ 67\text{ tens}}$. 2 tens x 30 = 60 tens, which is close to 67 tens. 7 tens are left. 2 tens x 3 = 6 tens, which leaves a remainder of 1 ten. $$33\ R\ 10$$ $20)\overline{670}$ -600 (20 x 30) $\quad\ 70$ $\ -60$ (20 x 3) $\quad\ 10$	Test Items: 6–7 Worksheet pages 57–59

PROBLEM TYPE	REMEDIATION	TEST ITEMS/WORKSHEETS

Dividing by Two-Digit Divisors
 	
$32\overline{)684}$
	Students should estimate the quotient by rounding the divisor to the nearest ten.
	
	$32\overline{)684}$
	
	Step 1: Round the divisor to 30.
	   3 tens x _____ is close to 68.
	
	Think:
	$3 \text{ tens}\overline{)68}$
	3 tens x 2 = 60
	60 < 68
	3 tens x 3 = 90
	90 > 68 (too much)
	Try 2.
	
	Step 2: Multiply: 32 x 2 = 64.
	   Write 64 under 68.
	
	$$\begin{array}{r} 2 \\ 32\overline{)684} \\ -\,64 \end{array}$$
		Test Items: 8–10
		
		Worksheet pages 60–62
		
		(Continued on page 50)

PROBLEM TYPE	REMEDIATION	TEST ITEMS/WORKSHEETS
Dividing by Two-Digit Divisors (continued from page 49)	**Step 3:** Subtract: 68 − 64 = 4. Then, bring down the 4 ones. $$\begin{array}{r} 2 \\ 32\overline{)684} \\ -\ 64\downarrow \\ \hline 44 \end{array}$$ **Step 4:** 32 x _____ is close to 44. $$\begin{array}{r} 2 \\ 32\overline{)684} \\ -\ 64 \\ \hline 44 \end{array}$$ ### Think: $$32\overline{)44}$$ 32 x 1 = 32 32 < 44 32 x 2 = 64 64 > 44 (too much) Try 1. **Step 5:** Multiply: 32 x 1 = 32. Write 32 under 44. $$\begin{array}{r} 21 \\ 32\overline{)684} \\ -\ 64 \\ \hline 44 \\ -\ 32 \end{array}$$ **Step 6:** Subtract to find the remainder. $$\begin{array}{r} 21\ R\ 12 \\ 32\overline{)684} \\ -\ 64 \\ \hline 44 \\ -\ 32 \\ \hline 12 \end{array}$$	Test Items: 8–10 Worksheet pages 60–62

CD-104227 • Jump Into Math • © Carson-Dellosa

Dividing Two Digits by One Digit

Dividing Two Digits by One Digit

Test Items 1–2

Directions: Study the example below. Then, solve the division problems.

Example: 3)89

Step 1: $8 \div 3 = 2$ R 2, so write a 2 over the tens place of the dividend. 2 tens x 3 = 60, so write 60 under the dividend.

Step 2: Subtract. $29 \div 3 = 9$ R 2, so write a 9 over the ones place of the dividend. 9 x 3 = 27, so write 27 under the dividend.

Step 3: Subtract to find the remainder.

```
     29 R 2
 3)89
   -60
    29
   -27
     2
```

1. 5)37

2. 5)24

3. 3)89

4. 3)49

5. 4)94

6. 9)91

7. 5)78

8. 7)33

9. 3)52

10. 4)65

11. 9)82

12. 5)62

Dividing Two Digits by One Digit Practice

Directions: Solve the division problems.

1. $5\overline{)33}$ 2. $6\overline{)58}$ 3. $8\overline{)66}$ 4. $6\overline{)94}$

5. $7\overline{)53}$ 6. $3\overline{)64}$ 7. $4\overline{)69}$ 8. $9\overline{)84}$

9. $97 \div 8 =$ _____ 10. $88 \div 5 =$ _____ 11. $79 \div 7 =$ _____

12. $85 \div 3 =$ _____ 13. $67 \div 3 =$ _____ 14. $84 \div 3 =$ _____

   CD-104227 • Jump Into Math • © Carson-Dellosa

More Dividing Two Digits by One Digit Practice

Directions: Circle the letter beside the number that will complete each number sentence.

1. $47 \div$ _____ $= 5\,R\,7$

   A. 6
   B. 7
   C. 8
   D. 9

2. $68 \div 8 =$ _____

   A. 5 R 2
   B. 6 R 4
   C. 77 R 1
   D. 8 R 4

3. $66 \div$ _____ $= 16\,R\,2$

   A. 4
   B. 5
   C. 6
   D. 7

4. $77 \div 5 =$ _____

   A. 12 R 5
   B. 15 R 2
   C. 15 R 4
   D. 18 R 2

5. $86 \div$ _____ $= 14\,R\,2$

   A. 4
   B. 5
   C. 6
   D. 7

6. $99 \div$ _____ $= 49\,R\,1$

   A. 2
   B. 3
   C. 4
   D. 5

7. $75 \div 8 =$ _____

   A. 6 R 5
   B. 7 R 4
   C. 8 R 2
   D. 9 R 3

8. $79 \div$ _____ $= 19\,R\,3$

   A. 4
   B. 5
   C. 6
   D. 7

9. $89 \div 3 =$ _____

   A. 27 R 3
   B. 28 R 2
   C. 29 R 2
   D. 30 R 1

Dividing Three Digits by One Digit

Directions: Study the example below. Then, divide the following problems.

Dividing Three Digits by One Digit	Place Value	Standard Algorithm
Step 1: Divide the hundreds.	$\begin{array}{r} 23\text{ R }3 \\ 5\overline{)118} \\ -100 \\ \hline 18 \\ -15 \\ \hline 3 \end{array}$	$\begin{array}{r} 23\text{ R }3 \\ 5\overline{)118} \\ -10\downarrow \\ \hline 18 \\ -15 \\ \hline 3 \end{array}$
Step 2: Divide the tens.		
Step 3: Divide the ones.		
Step 4: Find the remainder.		

1. $3\overline{)161}$ 2. $5\overline{)393}$ 3. $4\overline{)357}$ 4. $7\overline{)545}$

5. $6\overline{)254}$ 6. $7\overline{)533}$ 7. $4\overline{)360}$ 8. $8\overline{)638}$

9. $5\overline{)887}$ 10. $5\overline{)798}$ 11. $9\overline{)729}$ 12. $2\overline{)792}$

CD-104227 • Jump Into Math • © Carson-Dellosa

Dividing Four Digits by One Digit

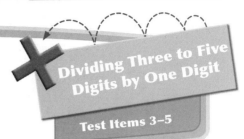

Dividing Three to Five Digits by One Digit

Test Items 3–5

Directions: Study the example below. Then, divide the following problems.

Dividing Four Digits by One Digit	Place Value	Standard Algorithm
Step 1: Divide the thousands.	2,146 R 1 2)4,293 −4 000 293	2,146 R 1 2)4,293 −4 02
Step 2: Divide the hundreds.	−200 93	− 2 09
Step 3: Divide the tens.	−80 13	− 8 13
Step 4: Divide the ones.	−12 1	−12 1
Step 5: Find the remainder.		

1. 3)4,982

2. 4)5,668

3. 5)7,807

4. 8)7,424

5. 9)7,548

6. 7)8,888

Dividing Five Digits by One Digit

Directions: Study the example below. Then, solve the division problems.

Dividing Five Digits by One Digit	Place Value	Standard Algorithm
Step 1: Divide the ten thousands.	2,470 R 1 5)12,351 − 10,000 2,351 −2,000 351 − 350 1 − 0 1	2,470 R 1 5)12,351 − 10↓ 23 −20↓ 35 − 35↓ 01 − 0 1
Step 2: Divide the thousands.		
Step 3: Divide the hundreds.		
Step 4: Divide the tens.		
Step 5: Divide the ones.		
Step 6: Find the remainder.		

1. 6)16,786

2. 4)29,586

3. 5)35,498

4. 8)54,703

5. 5)71,506

6. 7)46,835

CD-104227 • Jump Into Math • © Carson-Dellosa

Divide by Multiples of 10

Directions: Study the example below. Then, solve the division problems.

Example: 20)‾670‾

Think: 2 tens) 67 tens

2 tens x 30 = 60 tens
60 tens is close to 67 tens.
7 tens are left.

2 tens x 3 = 6 tens
6 tens is close to 7 tens.
1 ten is left as the remainder.

$$\begin{array}{r} 33\ R\ 10 \\ 20)\overline{670} \\ -600 \\ \hline 70 \\ -60 \\ \hline 10 \end{array}$$

1. 20)‾486‾

2. 30)‾665‾

3. 20)‾543‾

4. 30)‾361‾

5. 40)‾884‾

6. 30)‾937‾

7. 20)‾682‾

8. 40)‾725‾

9. 50)‾859‾

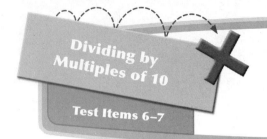

Practicing Division by Multiples of 10

Directions: Solve the division problems.

1. 10)7,780

2. 20)8,863

3. 30)6,543

4. 50)2,256

5. 40)3,326

6. 60)9,422

7. 40)5,600

8. 40)2,930

9. 50)7,510

10. 70)9,950

11. 90)6,485

12. 30)4,299

   CD-104227   •   Jump Into Math   •   © Carson-Dellosa

More Division by Multiples of 10

Dividing by Multiples of 10

Test Items 6–7

Directions: Solve each division problem below. Then, circle the letter beside the correct answer.

1. $10\overline{)925}$
   A. 92
   B. 92 R 5
   C. 93
   D. 90 R 5

2. $10\overline{)8,873}$
   A. 88 R 3
   B. 888
   C. 887
   D. 887 R 3

3. $10\overline{)680}$
   A. 68
   B. 608
   C. 680
   D. 68 R 8

4. $30\overline{)6,545}$
   A. 218 R 35
   B. 218 R 5
   C. 218 R 45
   D. 218 R 3

5. $50\overline{)1,700}$
   A. 32
   B. 34
   C. 304
   D. 340

6. $40\overline{)5,645}$
   A. 160 R 5
   B. 151 R 5
   C. 140 R 5
   D. 141 R 5

7. $60\overline{)8,947}$
   A. 149 R 4
   B. 149
   C. 149 R 7
   D. 194 R 7

8. $80\overline{)8,722}$
   A. 109 R 2
   B. 190 R 2
   C. 109 R 9
   D. 190 R 9

9. $40\overline{)4,346}$
   A. 18
   B. 18 R 26
   C. 108 R 26
   D. 180 R 26

10. $80\overline{)7,640}$
    A. 95 R 40
    B. 95 R 4
    C. 195 R 40
    D. 95

Divide by
Two-Digit Divisors

Directions: Solve the division problems below.

1. 25)655

2. 32)693

3. 42)848

4. 49)638

5. 39)845

6. 22)488

7. 52)619

8. 33)699

9. 43)989

10. 61)978

11. 48)730

12. 54)976

Practice Division by Two-Digit Divisors

Dividing by Two-Digit Divisors

Test Items 8–10

Directions: Solve the division problems below.

1. 18)3,679

2. 29)9,240

3. 23)4,649

4. 46)4,527

5. 37)9,998

6. 56)8,252

7. 52)5,538

8. 62)2,984

9. 67)8,752

10. 75)8,425

11. 81)8,807

12. 97)9,707

More Division by Two-Digit Divisors

Directions: Solve the division problems below.

1. $18\overline{)54{,}558}$

2. $19\overline{)46{,}854}$

3. $24\overline{)29{,}586}$

4. $48\overline{)56{,}261}$

5. $57\overline{)50{,}345}$

6. $67\overline{)92{,}929}$

7. $34\overline{)90{,}930}$

8. $61\overline{)27{,}458}$

9. $77\overline{)35{,}118}$

10. $81\overline{)77{,}077}$

11. $95\overline{)42{,}900}$

12. $99\overline{)87{,}245}$

Diagnostic Test:
Multiplication and Division of Decimals

Directions: Write your answer to each question in the space provided.

Part I: Multiplication of Decimals

1.   0.6
   x 9

6.   3.3
   x 2.5

2.   3.2
   x 3

7.   0.2
   x 0.3

3.   13.5 x 1,000 = _____

8.   2.46
   x 0.8

4.   10.25
   x 100

9.   3.05
   x 0.04

5.   5.45
   x 5

10.   2.165
   x 0.25

TEACHER ASSESSMENT AREA

Directions: Shade the boxes that correspond to correct test items.

Skill	Item Number				
Multiplying Decimals by Whole Numbers	1	2	3	4	5
Multiplying Decimals by Decimals	6	7	8	9	10

TOTAL CORRECT: _____

Teacher Notes and Activities

TEACHER NOTES: Multiplying Decimals by Whole Numbers
(Diagnostic Test Part I: Test Items 1–5)

Two of the most common errors students make when multiplying decimals by whole numbers are computation errors and incorrect placement of the decimal point in products. Students have practiced extensively with whole number multiplication, so computational errors should diminish by fifth grade. For students who still make computational errors, allow the use of multiplication tables. Errors in placement of the decimal point can be corrected by one of two methods: estimating the product and counting the number of decimal places in the factors.

TEACHING ACTIVITIES
"Decimal Placement" (Multiplying Decimals by Whole Numbers)

Instruct students to study the multiplication problem below.

$$\begin{array}{r} 0.9 \\ \times\ \ 8 \\ \hline \end{array}$$

Ask students to round 0.9 to the nearest whole number. Because 1 x 8 = 8, the product of 0.9 x 8 is close to 8.

$$\begin{array}{r} 1 \\ \times\ \ 8 \\ \hline 8 \end{array}$$

Instruct students to multiply, ignoring the decimal until the next step.

$$\begin{array}{r} 0.9 \\ \times\ \ 8 \\ \hline 72 \end{array}$$

Students should then use their estimate to place the decimal point. The decimal point belongs between the 7 and 2, because 7.2 is close to the estimated product (8).

$$\begin{array}{r} 0.9 \\ \times\ \ 8 \\ \hline 7.2 \end{array}$$

Another way to find where to place the decimal is to multiply, then count the total number of digits after the decimal point in each factor. That total is always equal to the number of digits after the decimal point in the product.

$$
\begin{array}{r} 0.9 \\ \times\ \ 8 \\ \hline 72 \end{array}
$$
1 digit after the decimal point.
0 digits after the decimal point.

$$
\begin{array}{r} 0.9 \\ \times\ \ 8 \\ \hline 7.2 \end{array}
$$
Count 1 digit and place the decimal.

Sometimes, it is necessary to add one or more zeros as placeholders. Demonstrate by solving the following example.

$$
\begin{array}{r} 0.009 \\ \times\ \ \ \ \ \ 8 \\ \hline 72 \end{array}
$$
Multiply.
Count the number of digits after the decimal in each factor.
The total is 3.

$$
\begin{array}{r} 0.009 \\ \times\ \ \ \ \ \ 8 \\ \hline 0.072 \end{array}
$$
There are only two digits in the product. Write a zero to hold the third place, then write the decimal point.

Adding zeros as placeholders can be difficult for some students. They may need additional demonstration, as well as individual practice.

"Multiplying by Multiples of 10" (Multiplying Decimals by Whole Numbers)

Multiplying a decimal by a multiple of 10 is as easy as moving the decimal point. When multiplying decimals by a multiple of 10, the number of zeros in the multiple of 10 indicates how many places to the right to move the decimal point. Add and take away placeholder zeros as needed. Review the examples below with students.

13.5	1 x 13.5 = 13.5 10 x 13.5 = 135 (move the decimal 1 place to the right) 100 x 13.5 = 1,350 (move the decimal 2 places to the right) 1,000 x 13.5 = 13,500 (move the decimal 3 places to the right)
0.005	1 x 0.005 = 0.005 10 x 0.005 = 0.05 (move the decimal 1 place to the right) 100 x 0.005 = 0.5 (move the decimal 2 places to the right) 1,000 x 0.005 = 5 (move the decimal 3 places to the right)

TEACHER NOTES: Multiplying Decimals by Decimals

(Diagnostic Test Part I: Test Items 6–10)

The same methods used to teach multiplication of decimals by whole numbers can be used to teach multiplication of decimals by decimals. Again, common errors include computational errors and misplacement of the decimal point in products.

TEACHING ACTIVITIES

"Estimate the Product" (Multiplying Decimals by Decimals)

Step 1: Round each factor to the nearest whole number.	5.2 x 3.5 is close to 5 x 4
Step 2: Multiply the whole numbers.	5 x 4 = 20
Step 3: Multiply, ignoring the decimals until the next step.	5.2 x 3.5 260 + 1560 1820
Step 4: Use your estimate to place the decimal point. **Think:** 18.20 is close to 20.	**18.20**

"Count the Decimal Places" (Multiplying Decimals by Decimals)

Step 1: Multiply, ignoring the decimals until the next step.	5.2 x 3.5 260 + 1560 1820
Step 2: Count the digits after the decimals in the factors.	5.**2** x 3.**5** 260 + 1560 1820
Step 3: Write the decimal in the product according to how many digits come after the decimal points in the factors.	5.2 x 3.5 260 + 1560 18.20

"Two Methods Are Better Than One" (Multiplying Decimals by Decimals)

Step 1: Estimate the product.	1.243 x 2.8 1 x 3 = 3
Step 2: Multiply, ignoring the decimals until the next step.	1.243 x 2.8 9944 + 24860 34804
Step 3: Count the digits after the decimals in the factors. Write the decimal in the product according to the total.	1.243 (3 digits) x 2.8 (1 digit) 9944 + 24860 3.4804 (4 digits total)
Step 4: Check your answer.	Is 3.4804 close to 3? Yes.

Instruct students to practice the estimation method and the counting the decimal places method with the problems below.

1.   0.29
   x 0.05

2.   18.1
   x 0.25

3.   3.54
   x 2.8

4.   2.156
   x 0.25

5.   0.8
   x 0.8

6.   0.006
   x 0.5

7.   3.65
   x 0.7

8.   23.06
   x 0.23

Estimate to Place the Decimal

Directions: Study the example. Then, solve the multiplication problems.

Example: 0.9
          x 8

1. Round 0.9 to the nearest whole number (1). Because
    1 x 8 = 8, the product of 0.9 x 8 is close to 8.

2. Multiply, ignoring the decimal points until the next step.

3. The estimated product is close to 8. So, the decimal
    point goes between the 7 and 2.

    0.9 x 8 = 7.2

1.   1
    x 8
    ———
      8

2.   0.9
    x 8
    ———
     72

3.   0.9
    x 8
    ———
    7.2

---

1.   0.6
    x 6

2.   0.5
    x 5

3.   0.8
    x 7

4.   0.3
    x 7

5.   0.9
    x 7

6.   0.2
    x 9

7.   0.3
    x 8

8.   0.6
    x 7

9.   0.4
    x 7

10.   0.6
     x 8

11.   1 2
     x 0.4

12.   1 5
     x 0.9

13.   2 3
     x 0.6

14.   1 8
     x 0.5

15.   3.3
     x 8

16.   3.2
     x 3

NAME: _____   DATE: _____

Counting Decimal Places

Multiplying Decimals by Whole Numbers

Test Items 1–5

Directions: Study the example. Then, solve the multiplication problems.

Example: Count the decimal places in the factors. That number is the number of digits that should be to the right of the decimal point in the product. Sometimes, you must write a zero or zeros as placeholders in the product.

0.009	Multiply 8 x 9.	0.009	There are only two digits in the
x 8	Count the number of digits after the	x 8	product. Write a zero to hold
72	decimal in each factor.	**0.072**	the third place. Then, write the
	The total is 3.		decimal point.

1. 0.07	2. 0.008	3. 0.09	4. 0.005
x 9	x 9	x 9	x 9

5. 0.33	6. 0.53	7. 0.47	8. 0.65
x 8	x 3	x 5	x 6

9. 0.006	10. 0.082	11. 0.91	12. 0.76
x 7	x 4	x 7	x 9

13. 0.68	14. 8 6	15. 7 5	16. 9 9
x 7	x 0.9	x 0.7	x 0.8

Multiplying
Decimals by
Whole Numbers

Test Items 1–5

Decimals and Multiplies of 10

Directions: Study the examples. Then, solve the multiplication problems.

Example: When multiplying by a multiple of 10, the number of zeros in the multiple of 10 shows you how many places to move the decimal point to the right.

13.5
1 x 13.5 = 13.5
10 x 13.5 = 135 (move the decimal 1 place to the right)
100 x 13.5 = 1,350 (move the decimal 2 places to the right)
1,000 x 13.5 = 13,500 (move the decimal 3 places to the right)

0.005
1 x 0.005 = 0.005
10 x 0.005 = 0.05 (move the decimal 1 place to the right)
100 x 0.005 = 0.5 (move the decimal 2 places to the right)
1,000 x 0.005 = 5 (move the decimal 3 places to the right)

1. 10 x 0.25 = _____

2. 10 x 1.35 = _____

3. 10 x 3.45 = _____

4. 10 x 4.37 = _____

5. 10 x 6.13 = _____

6. 10 x 8.58 = _____

7. 100 x 0.25 = _____

8. 100 x 4.35 = _____

9. 100 x 5.38 = _____

10. 100 x 66.6 = _____

11. 100 x 79.3 = _____

12. 100 x 82.3 = _____

13. 1,000 x 0.25 = _____

14. 1,000 x 3.49 = _____

15. 1,000 x 9.61 = _____

16. 1,000 x 86.4 = _____

17. 1,000 x 77.6 = _____

18. 1,000 x 92.5 = _____

NAME: _____ DATE: _____

How Many Decimal Places?

Directions: Study the example. Then, solve the multiplication problems.

Example:

5.2 x 3.5

1. Multiply, ignoring the decimals until the next step.

2. Count the decimal places in the factors. Write the decimal in the product that many places to the left.

5.2 x 3.5 = 18.20

```
1.     5.2        2.     5.2
     x 3.5             x 3.5
     ─────            ─────
      260              260
    +1560            +1560
     ─────            ─────
     1820            18.20
```

1.   5.3
     x 2.8

2.   4.9
     x 0.2

3.   8.8
     x 4.3

4.   0.56
     x 0.05

5.   0.75
     x 0.75

6.   0.68
     x 0.59

7.   0.013
     x 0.43

8.   24.1
     x 0.14

9.   26.2
     x 7.8

10.   61.8
     x 0.7

11.   4.92
     x 0.35

12.   5.21
     x 0.75

Multiplying
Decimals
by Decimals

Test Items 6–10

Check Your Answers with Estimates

Directions: Study the example. Then, solve the multiplication problems.

Example: **1.243 x 2.8**

1. Estimate the product.

2. Count the decimal places in the factors. Put that number of decimal places in the product.

3. Check your answer with your estimate.

1.243 x 2.8 = 3.4804

1. 1.243 x 2.8   1 x 3 = **3**

2.
```
    1.243
  x   2.8
    9944
 + 24860
  3.4804
```

3. 3.4804 is close to 3.

1. 15.3
    x 2.34

2. 3.08
    x 5.3

3. 35.6
    x 0.42

4. 9.17
    x 3.4

5. 1.405
    x 0.6

6. 5.03
    x 6.8

7. 5.78
    x 2.1

8. 15.3
    x 2.34

9. 6.02
    x 0.04

10. 47.6
     x 0.042

11. 7.81
     x 15.2

12. 0.149
     x 0.53

Placing Decimals

Multiplying
Decimals
by Decimals
Test Items 6–10

Directions: Write the combined number of decimals places in each set of factors. Then, place the decimal in the correct position for each product and solve the last three multiplication problems. The first row has been done for you.

FACTORS	NUMBER OF DECIMAL PLACES IN THE FACTORS	PLACE THE DECIMAL IN THE PRODUCT.
1. 17.17 x 0.147	5	2.52399
2. 11.47 x 6.55		751185
3. 25.28 x 0.033		083424
4. 31.31 x 0.33		103333
5. 23.06 x 0.23		053038
6. 23.92 x 3.63		868296
7. 37.36 x 0.18		69248
8. 46.54 x 0.25		11635
9. 27.43 x 81.6		2238288
10. 19.89 x 2.76		
11. 20.89 x 0.36		
12. 53.31 x 0.44		

Diagnostic Test:
Multiplication and Division of Decimals

Directions: Write your answer to each question in the space provided. Round each answer to the nearest thousandth.

Part II: Division

1. $2\overline{)6.60}$

2. $9\overline{)7.38}$

3. $5\overline{)9.67}$

4. $64\overline{)768.8}$

5. $31\overline{)421.6}$

6. $6.8\overline{)4.76}$

7. $3.8\overline{)4.25}$

8. $2.5\overline{)8.50}$

9. $3.25\overline{)16.40}$

10. $2.13\overline{)45.70}$

TEACHER ASSESSMENT AREA

Directions: Shade the boxes that correspond to correct test items.

Skill			Item Number		
Dividing Decimals by Whole Numbers	1	2	3	4	5
Dividing Decimals by Decimals	6	7	8	9	10

TOTAL CORRECT:_____

CD-104227 • Jump Into Math • © Carson-Dellosa

Teacher Notes and Activities

TEACHER NOTES: Division of Decimals

(Diagnostic Test Part II: Test Items 1–10)

Division of decimals is very similar to division of whole numbers. Dividing decimals requires only the standard division algorithm together with a method for placing the decimal point. Convey this idea to students so that they see that they are not learning a new algorithm, just a small change to the one they already know.

TEACHING ACTIVITIES

"Dividing Decimals by Whole Numbers" (Division of Decimals)

To divide a decimal by a whole number, perform the division as if the dividend is a whole number. Then, place the decimal point in the quotient directly above the decimal point in the dividend.

Example 1:

$$11.65 \div 5$$

Perform long division as if there is no decimal point in the dividend.

```
      233
  5)11.65
    -10
     16
    -15
     15
    -15
      0
```

Then, insert the decimal point in the quotient directly above the decimal point in the dividend.

```
     2.33
  5)11.65
```

$$11.65 \div 5 = 2.33$$

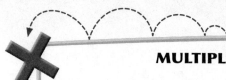

Example 2:

$$6.35 \div 4$$

Perform long division as if there is no decimal point in the dividend. Write zeros in the dividend so that there are enough digits to complete division without leaving a remainder.

```
        15875
   4)6.3500
     -4
      23
     -20
       35
      -32
        30
       -28
         20
        -20
          0
```

Then, insert the decimal point in the quotient directly above the decimal point in the dividend.

```
     1.5875
  4)6.3500
```

$$6.35 \div 4 = 1.5875$$

"Dividing a Decimal by a Decimal" (Division of Decimals)

To divide a decimal by a decimal, multiply both the divisor and the dividend by a multiple of 10 to make the divisor a whole number. This may require adding zeros to the end of the dividend as placeholders.

CAN'T DIVIDE:		CAN DIVIDE:
2.6)5.2	(x 10)	26)52
2.68)5.23	(x 100)	268)523
2.681)5.238	(x 1,000)	2,681)5,238

MULTIPLICATION AND DIVISION OF DECIMALS
PART II: DIVISION

Before asking students to perform this type of division, instruct them to practice "moving" the decimal points (multiplying by a 10 or 100) in the problems below.

1. 8)5.40

2. 0.21)4.3

3. 4.11)34.12

Then, walk students through the steps for solving a decimal division problem.

STEP 1:	STEP 2:	STEP 3:	STEP 4:
Write the problem in division house form.	Move the decimal points in the divisor and the dividend to the right until the divisor becomes a whole number.	Perform division as usual.	Place a decimal point in the quotient directly above the decimal point in the dividend.
14.292 ÷ 0.12			
0.12)14.292	12)1,429.2	119 1 12)1,429.2 − 12 22 −12 109 −108 12 −12 0	119.1 12)1,429.2 **14.292 ÷ 0.12 = 119.1**

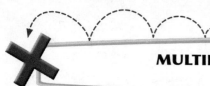

STEP 1:

Write the problem in division house form.

346.5 ÷ 0.25

$$0.25\overline{)346.5}$$

STEP 2:

Move the decimal points in the divisor and the dividend to the right until the divisor becomes a whole number. Add a zero to the end of the dividend so that the decimal point can be moved two places to the right.

$$25\overline{)34650}$$

STEP 3:

Perform division as usual. Because the divisor, dividend, and quotient are all whole numbers, a decimal point is not needed.

$$
\begin{array}{r}
1,386 \\
25\overline{)34,650} \\
-\ 25 \\
\hline
96 \\
-\ 75 \\
\hline
215 \\
-\ 200 \\
\hline
150 \\
-\ 150 \\
\hline
0
\end{array}
$$

SPECIAL TEACHER NOTE

Many division problems will have a quotient that has a long decimal or a repeating decimal. Students should generally divide and round the quotient to the nearest thousandth.

REPEATING DECIMAL

$$
\begin{array}{r}
22.27272727... \\
3.3\overline{)75}
\end{array}
$$

Round to the nearest thousandth: 22.273

A repeating decimal can also be written with a bar above the repeating digits: $22.\overline{27}$.

LONG DECIMAL

$$
\begin{array}{r}
0.42857142857 \\
70\overline{)30}
\end{array}
$$

Round to the nearest thousandth: 0.429

CD-104227 • Jump Into Math • © Carson-Dellosa

Keep the Decimal in Place

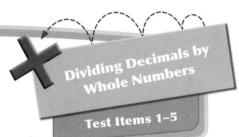

Dividing Decimals by Whole Numbers

Test Items 1–5

Directions: Study the example. Then, solve the division problems.

Example:

11.65 ÷ 5

Perform division as if there is no decimal point in the dividend.

$$\begin{array}{r} 233 \\ 5\overline{)11.65} \\ -10 \\ \hline 16 \\ -15 \\ \hline 15 \\ -15 \\ \hline 0 \end{array}$$

Then, write a decimal point in the quotient directly above the decimal point in the dividend.

$$\begin{array}{r} 2.33 \\ 5\overline{)11.65} \end{array}$$

11.65 ÷ 5 = 2.33

1. $4\overline{)2.92}$

2. $4\overline{)4.64}$

3. $5\overline{)6.35}$

4. $3\overline{)5.25}$

5. $4\overline{)6.68}$

6. $5\overline{)9.65}$

7. $8\overline{)4.65}$

8. $9\overline{)4.86}$

Practicing Division

Directions: Solve the division problems.

1. $15\overline{)8.25}$

2. $33\overline{)181.5}$

3. $13\overline{)356.2}$

4. $31\overline{)421.6}$

5. $44\overline{)558.8}$

6. $32\overline{)195.2}$

7. $15\overline{)38.85}$

8. $12\overline{)150.60}$

9. $43\overline{)15.05}$

10. $78\overline{)257.4}$

11. $19\overline{)10.45}$

12. $64\overline{)206.08}$

Word Problems with Decimals

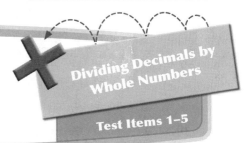

Dividing Decimals by Whole Numbers

Test Items 1–5

Directions: Solve the division word problems. Show your work. Use a separate sheet of paper if needed.

1. Clayton earned $160.80 last week working at his uncle's bookstore. If he worked for 24 hours, how much did he earn per hour?

    _____

2. Laney's mother gave her $12.50 for her 5 school lunches this week. How much can she spend on each lunch?

    _____

3. Mr. Jackson's art class, which consists of 32 students, bought him a gift that totaled $195.20. The students split the cost of the gift equally. How much did each student pay?

    _____

4. The Hwang family paid a total of $33.75 for their movie tickets. There are 5 members in the family and each ticket was the same price. How much did each movie ticket cost?

    _____

5. The Garcias' 3 children spent $21.66 on soda and popcorn. If each child spent the same amount, how much did each child spend on refreshments?

    _____

6. Mrs. Dotson spent $38.85 on assorted cheese, which cost $2.59 per pound. How many pounds of cheese did she buy?

    _____

NAME: _____   DATE: _____

Decimal Division

Directions: Study the examples below. Then, solve the division problems.

Example: To divide a decimal by a decimal, multiply both the divisor and the dividend by a multiple of 10 to make the divisor a whole number. This may require adding zeros to the end of the dividend as placeholders. Then, divide.

CAN'T DIVIDE:		CAN DIVIDE:
$2.6\overline{)5.2}$	(x 10)	$26\overline{)52}$
$2.68\overline{)5.23}$	(x 100)	$268\overline{)523}$
$2.681\overline{)5.238}$	(x 1000)	$2681\overline{)5238}$

1. $7.2\overline{)9.72}$

2. $3.8\overline{)5.32}$

3. $6.8\overline{)4.76}$

4. $2.1\overline{)6.93}$

5. $2.5\overline{)8.50}$

6. $0.03\overline{)92.1}$

7. $0.34\overline{)0.782}$

8. $1.24\overline{)76.88}$

9. $0.016\overline{)0.192}$

More Decimal Division

Directions: Solve the division problems. Round to the nearest thousandth.

1. $3.8\overline{)4.25}$

2. $0.64\overline{)4.672}$

3. $5.04\overline{)46.368}$

4. $1.24\overline{)76.88}$

5. $2.11\overline{)14.348}$

6. $2.04\overline{)113.22}$

7. $0.25\overline{)346.50}$

8. $0.016\overline{)0.176}$

9. $0.015\overline{)0.285}$

10. $12\overline{)0.144}$

11. $0.940\overline{)2.256}$

12. $0.099\overline{)8.811}$

Practicing
Decimal Division

Directions: Solve the division problems. Use the space provided to show your work.

1. $25.92 \div 0.04 =$ _____

2. $35.01 \div 0.09 =$ _____

3. $54.08 \div 0.08 =$ _____

4. $202.35 \div 0.57 =$ _____

5. $87.95 \div 0.05 =$ _____

6. $23.92 \div 0.78 =$ _____

7. $185.6 \div 3.2 =$ _____

8. $1,125.2 \div 9.7 =$ _____

CD-104227 • Jump Into Math • © Carson-Dellosa

Diagnostic Test:
Addition and Subtraction of Fractions

Directions: Write your answer to each question in the space provided. Use another sheet of paper to show your work, if necessary.

Part I: Addition

1. $\dfrac{1}{4} + \dfrac{5}{12} =$

2. $\dfrac{5}{8} + \dfrac{4}{9} =$

3. $\dfrac{3}{8} + \dfrac{5}{6} =$

4. $\dfrac{3}{16} + \dfrac{5}{6} =$

5. $\dfrac{4}{15} + \dfrac{5}{12} =$

6. $4\dfrac{3}{5} + 2\dfrac{3}{4} =$

7. $\begin{array}{r} 2\dfrac{1}{3} \\ + \ 5\dfrac{1}{5} \\ \hline \end{array}$

8. $3\dfrac{2}{3} + 4\dfrac{5}{6} =$

9. $3\dfrac{1}{4} + 5\dfrac{5}{6} =$

10. $\begin{array}{r} 2\dfrac{1}{3} \\ + \ 2\dfrac{3}{5} \\ \hline \end{array}$

TEACHER ASSESSMENT AREA

Directions: Shade the boxes that correspond to correct test items.

Skill	Item Number				
Adding Unlike Denominators	1	2	3	4	5
Adding Mixed Numbers	6	7	8	9	10

TOTAL CORRECT: _____

Teacher Notes and Activities

ADDITION AND SUBTRACTION OF FRACTIONS PART I: ADDITION

TEACHER NOTES: Adding Unlike Denominators
(Diagnostic Test Part I: Test Items 1–5)

Adding fractions with unlike denominators is a review skill for most fifth-grade students. A troublesome area for students is finding the lowest common multiple (LCM) in order to convert fractions to equivalent fractions with the lowest common denominator (LCD). Review this process before teaching students how to add fractions with unlike denominators.

TEACHING ACTIVITIES
"Finding the LCM" (Adding Unlike Denominators)

Before students can add a pair of fractions with unlike denominators, they must find common denominators and convert one or both fractions to make a pair of equivalent fractions. Practice finding common multiples of pairs of numbers. Common multiples are multiples that are the same for two or more numbers. The lowest common multiple (LCM) is the smallest common multiple for each pair of numbers.

Explain to students that to find the LCM of two numbers, they must list the multiples of both numbers. Then, they should circle the smallest common multiple.

> Find the multiples for each number. Then, circle the LCM in each pair.
>
> **3:** 3   6   9   12   (15)   **6:** 6   12   18   (24)
>
> **5:** 5   10   (15)   **8:** 8   16   (24)

Use number cards or dice to generate pairs of numbers. Students should write 5–10 multiples of each number and circle the LCM for each pair.

"Finding the LCD" (Adding Unlike Denominators)

Explain to students that to find the lowest common denominator (LCD) for two fractions, they must write a list of multiples of each denominator. Then, they should circle the lowest common multiple. This is the lowest common denominator (LCD).

Find the lowest common denominator (LCD) for each pair of fractions.

$\frac{1}{3}$ and $\frac{1}{4}$

3:   3   6   9   ⑫

4:   4   8   ⑫

LCD = **12**

$\frac{1}{6}$ and $\frac{1}{8}$

6:   6   12   18   ㉔

8:   8   16   ㉔

LCD = **24**

Demonstrate how to use the lowest common denominator to add the following fractions.

$\frac{1}{3}$ + $\frac{1}{4}$

Convert each fraction to an equivalent fraction with the lowest common denominator of 12.

$$\frac{1}{3} \times \frac{4}{4} = \frac{4}{12} \qquad \frac{1}{4} \times \frac{3}{3} = \frac{3}{12}$$

Then, add the equivalent fractions:

$$\frac{4}{12} + \frac{3}{12} = \frac{7}{12}$$

$\frac{1}{6}$ + $\frac{1}{8}$

Convert each fraction to an equivalent fraction with the lowest common denominator of 24.

$$\frac{1}{6} \times \frac{4}{4} = \frac{4}{24} \qquad \frac{1}{8} \times \frac{3}{3} = \frac{3}{24}$$

Then, add the equivalent fractions:

$$\frac{4}{24} + \frac{3}{24} = \frac{7}{24}$$

Explain to students that they can always multiply the denominators to find a common multiple.

$$\frac{1}{5} \quad + \quad \frac{1}{7}$$

Multiply the denominators: 5 x 7 = 35. Convert each fraction to an equivalent fraction with a common denominator of 35.

$$\frac{1}{5} \quad \times \quad \frac{7}{7} \quad = \quad \frac{7}{35} \qquad\qquad \frac{1}{7} \quad \times \quad \frac{5}{5} \quad = \quad \frac{5}{35}$$

Then, add the equivalent fractions:

$$\frac{7}{35} \quad + \quad \frac{5}{35} \quad = \quad \frac{12}{35}$$

TEACHER NOTES: Adding Mixed Numbers
(Diagnostic Test Part I: Test Items 6–10)

Adding mixed fractions uses the same procedure for adding fractions with like and unlike denominators, as well as for the additional step of adding whole numbers. If students are proficient with adding like and unlike denominators, adding mixed fractions should not be difficult.

TEACHING DEMONSTRATION

Students should follow the steps below to add mixed numbers:

$$2 \frac{1}{2} \quad + \quad 6 \frac{3}{4} \quad =$$

Step 1: Rewrite the problem in vertical form. Convert the fractions using the LCD.

Step 2: Add the whole numbers. Then, add the fractions.

$$2 \frac{1}{2} = 2 \frac{2}{4}$$
$$6 \frac{3}{4} = 6 \frac{3}{4}$$

$$\longrightarrow$$

$$2 \frac{2}{4}$$
$$+ \quad 6 \frac{3}{4}$$
$$8 \frac{5}{4}$$

Step 3: Simplify the answer.

$$2 \frac{2}{4}$$
$$+ \quad 6 \frac{3}{4}$$

$$8 \frac{5}{4} = 8 + 1 \frac{1}{4} = 9 \frac{1}{4}$$

In the next example, both fractions must be converted.

$$4 \frac{6}{9} + 6 \frac{1}{2} =$$

Step 1: Rewrite the problem in vertical form.
Convert the fractions using the LCD.

$$4 \frac{6}{9} = 4 \frac{12}{18}$$
$$+ \quad 6 \frac{1}{2} = 6 \frac{9}{18}$$

Step 2: Add the whole numbers. Then, add the fractions.

$$4 \frac{12}{18}$$
$$+ \quad 6 \frac{9}{18}$$

$$10 \frac{21}{18}$$

Step 3: Simplify the answer.

$$4 \frac{12}{18}$$
$$+ \quad 6 \frac{9}{18}$$

$$10 \frac{21}{18} = 10 + 1 \frac{3}{18} = 11 \frac{1}{6}$$

$$4 \frac{6}{9} + 6 \frac{1}{2} = 11 \frac{1}{6}$$

NAME: _____ DATE: _____

Find the Lowest Common Denominator

Directions: List the multiples of each denominator. Circle the lowest common multiple. This is the lowest common denominator (LCD) for the two fractions. Write the LCD on the line.

$\frac{1}{2}$:   2   4   ⑥   8   10

$\frac{2}{3}$:   3   ⑥   9   12   15

LCD = **6**

1. $\frac{1}{3}$: ___ ___ ___ ___ ___

   $\frac{2}{5}$: ___ ___ ___ ___ ___

   LCD = _____

2. $\frac{1}{2}$: ___ ___ ___ ___ ___

   $\frac{3}{4}$: ___ ___ ___ ___ ___

   LCD = _____

3. $\frac{5}{6}$: ___ ___ ___ ___ ___ ___

   $\frac{2}{7}$: ___ ___ ___ ___ ___ ___

   LCD = _____

4. $\frac{1}{4}$: ___ ___ ___ ___ ___

   $\frac{4}{5}$: ___ ___ ___ ___ ___

   LCD = _____

5. $\frac{1}{3}$: ___ ___ ___ ___ ___

   $\frac{1}{4}$: ___ ___ ___ ___ ___

   LCD = _____

6. $\frac{2}{3}$: ___ ___ ___ ___ ___

   $\frac{3}{8}$: ___ ___ ___ ___ ___

   LCD = _____

NAME: _____   DATE: _____

Adding with a lowest common denominator

Adding Unlike Denominators

Test Items 1–5

Directions: Find the lowest common denominator (LCD). Then, change each pair of fractions to equivalents using the LCD. Add the equivalent fractions. Write each sum in simplest form.

Example: Find the lowest common denominator for each pair of fractions.

$\dfrac{1}{3}$ + $\dfrac{1}{4}$

3:   3   6   9   ⑫

4:   4   8   ⑫

LCD = 12

Convert fractions to equivalent fractions with the lowest common denominator of 12.

$\dfrac{1}{3}$ x $\dfrac{4}{4}$ = $\dfrac{4}{12}$ $\dfrac{1}{4}$ x $\dfrac{3}{3}$ = $\dfrac{3}{12}$

Then, add the equivalent fractions: $\dfrac{4}{12}$ + $\dfrac{3}{12}$ = $\dfrac{7}{12}$

1. $\dfrac{1}{2}$ + $\dfrac{5}{6}$ =

2. $\dfrac{2}{9}$ + $\dfrac{3}{6}$ =

3. $\dfrac{3}{4}$ + $\dfrac{11}{12}$ =

4. $\dfrac{4}{9}$ + $\dfrac{1}{2}$ =

5. $\dfrac{2}{3}$ + $\dfrac{3}{4}$ =

6. $\dfrac{3}{5}$ + $\dfrac{1}{2}$ =

7. $\dfrac{4}{5}$ + $\dfrac{3}{6}$ =

8. $\dfrac{4}{7}$ + $\dfrac{1}{2}$ =

9. $\dfrac{5}{7}$ + $\dfrac{1}{3}$ =

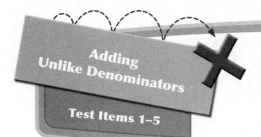

Fraction Addition Practice

Directions: Use the lowest common denominator (LCD) to make each pair of fractions equivalent. Then, add and write the sum in simplest form.

1. $\dfrac{1}{2} + \dfrac{5}{10} =$　　2. $\dfrac{2}{4} + \dfrac{2}{3} =$　　3. $\dfrac{6}{7} + \dfrac{1}{2} =$

4. $\dfrac{2}{3} + \dfrac{3}{5} =$　　5. $\dfrac{7}{9} + \dfrac{2}{3} =$　　6. $\dfrac{4}{5} + \dfrac{1}{2} =$

7. $\dfrac{1}{8} + \dfrac{1}{4} =$　　8. $\dfrac{5}{8} + \dfrac{1}{2} =$　　9. $\dfrac{3}{4} + \dfrac{5}{6} =$

10. $\dfrac{5}{6} + \dfrac{1}{2} =$　　11. $\dfrac{7}{8} + \dfrac{2}{4} =$　　12. $\dfrac{3}{5} + \dfrac{8}{10} =$

13. $\dfrac{4}{9} + \dfrac{1}{3} =$　　14. $\dfrac{1}{6} + \dfrac{8}{12} =$　　15. $\dfrac{5}{7} + \dfrac{1}{2} =$

16. $\dfrac{3}{4} + \dfrac{5}{8} =$　　17. $\dfrac{2}{6} + \dfrac{1}{2} =$　　18. $\dfrac{1}{2} + \dfrac{4}{8} =$

CD-104227 • Jump Into Math • © Carson-Dellosa

Lining Up Mixed Numbers

Adding
Mixed Numbers

Test Items 6–10

Directions: Study the example. Then, solve the addition problems.

Example:

$$2\frac{1}{2} + 6\frac{3}{4}$$

Step 1: Rewrite each problem in vertical form. Then, make the fractions equivalent.

$$2\frac{1}{2} = 2\frac{2}{4}$$
$$+\ 6\frac{3}{4} = 6\frac{3}{4}$$

Step 2: Add the whole numbers. Then, add the fractions.

$$2\frac{1}{2} = 2\frac{2}{4}$$
$$+\ 6\frac{3}{4} = 6\frac{3}{4}$$
$$8\frac{5}{4}$$

Step 3: Simplify.

$$2\frac{1}{2} = 2\frac{2}{4}$$
$$+\ 6\frac{3}{4} = 6\frac{3}{4}$$
$$8\frac{5}{4} = 9\frac{1}{4}$$

1. $2\frac{2}{3} + 4\frac{1}{2} =$

2. $4\frac{3}{5} + 3\frac{5}{10} =$

3. $6\frac{1}{3} + 2\frac{6}{9} =$

4. $7\frac{1}{3} + 2\frac{1}{2} =$

5. $4\frac{6}{7} + 4\frac{1}{2} =$

6. $3\frac{1}{2} + 4\frac{1}{5} =$

Practice with Mixed Numbers

Directions: Study the example. Then, solve the addition problems.

Example:

$$4\frac{6}{9} + 6\frac{1}{2}$$

$$4\frac{6}{9} = 4\frac{12}{18}$$

Make the fractions equivalent.

$$+\ 6\frac{1}{2} = 6\frac{9}{18}$$

Add whole numbers. Then, add fractions.

Simplify.

$$10\frac{21}{18} = 10 + 1\frac{3}{18} = 11\frac{3}{18} = 11\frac{1}{6}$$

1. $4\frac{3}{9} + 5\frac{1}{6} =$

2. $7\frac{3}{9} + 5\frac{1}{2} =$

3. $2\frac{2}{5} + 3\frac{1}{2} =$

4. $1\frac{6}{7} + 5\frac{1}{3} =$

5. $1\frac{6}{8} + 6\frac{1}{3} =$

6. $4\frac{3}{4} + 4\frac{7}{12} =$

7. $7\frac{2}{3} + 3\frac{7}{9} =$

8. $1\frac{4}{7} + 5\frac{1}{3} =$

More Mixed Number Practice

Adding
Mixed Numbers

Test Items 6–10

Directions: Solve the addition problems.

1. $2 \dfrac{5}{9} + 6 \dfrac{2}{3} =$

2. $5 \dfrac{1}{2} + 3 \dfrac{1}{8} =$

3. $4 \dfrac{6}{9} + 6 \dfrac{1}{2} =$

4. $5 \dfrac{4}{6} + 6 \dfrac{2}{4} =$

5. $2 \dfrac{3}{5} + 3 \dfrac{1}{3} =$

6. $4 \dfrac{4}{6} + 3 \dfrac{1}{3} =$

7. $5 \dfrac{5}{7} + 2 \dfrac{1}{2} =$

8. $3 \dfrac{3}{9} + 4 \dfrac{2}{3} =$

Diagnostic Test:
Addition and Subtraction of Fractions

Directions: Write your answer to each question in the space provided.

Part II: Subtraction

1. $\dfrac{7}{8} - \dfrac{1}{6} =$

2. $\dfrac{5}{6} - \dfrac{1}{4} =$

3. $\dfrac{9}{10} - \dfrac{3}{5} =$

4. $\begin{array}{r} \dfrac{6}{8} \\[6pt] -\ \dfrac{1}{2} \\ \hline \end{array}$

5. $\begin{array}{r} \dfrac{3}{4} \\[6pt] -\ \dfrac{3}{10} \\ \hline \end{array}$

6. $3\dfrac{5}{7} - 1\dfrac{1}{2} =$

7. $6\dfrac{1}{5} - 1\dfrac{1}{2} =$

8. $6\dfrac{2}{8} - 2\dfrac{1}{2} =$

9. $\begin{array}{r} 5\dfrac{1}{2} \\[6pt] -\ 3\dfrac{4}{9} \\ \hline \end{array}$

10. $\begin{array}{r} 3\dfrac{1}{2} \\[6pt] -\ 1\dfrac{3}{7} \\ \hline \end{array}$

TEACHER ASSESSMENT AREA

Directions: Shade the boxes that correspond to correct test items.

Skill	Item Number				
Subtracting Unlike Denominators	1	2	3	4	5
Subtracting Mixed Numbers	6	7	8	9	10

TOTAL CORRECT: _____

Teacher Notes and Activities

TEACHER NOTES: Subtracting Unlike Denominators

(Diagnostic Test Part II: Test Items 1–5)

Teach subtraction with unlike denominators alongside addition. These skills are review for fifth-grade students. The procedure for finding the lowest common denominator is the same for both addition and subtraction with unlike denominators.

TEACHING DEMONSTRATION

You can use the same demonstration activity listed in the previous section on addition with unlike denominators to teach subtraction. The process for finding the lowest common denominator (LCD) applies to subtraction as well. Demonstrate the subtraction process using the examples below.

$$\frac{1}{3} - \frac{1}{4}$$

Convert the fractions to equivalent fractions with an LCD of 12.

$$\frac{1}{3} \times \frac{4}{4} = \frac{4}{12} \qquad\qquad \frac{1}{4} \times \frac{3}{3} = \frac{3}{12}$$

Then, subtract the equivalent fractions.

$$\frac{4}{12} - \frac{3}{12} = \frac{1}{12}$$

$$\frac{7}{8} - \frac{1}{6}$$

Convert the fractions to equivalent fractions with an LCD of 24.

$$\frac{7}{8} \times \frac{3}{3} = \frac{21}{24} \qquad\qquad \frac{1}{6} \times \frac{4}{4} = \frac{4}{24}$$

Then, subtract the equivalent fractions.

$$\frac{21}{24} - \frac{4}{24} = \frac{17}{24}$$

Students should practice finding the LCD for each pair of fractions below. Instruct them to perform subtraction after they find the lowest common denominator. Remind them to write answers in simplest form.

1.

$$\frac{5}{6}$$
$$-\frac{1}{4}$$

2.

$$\frac{9}{10}$$
$$-\frac{3}{5}$$

3.

$$\frac{4}{5}$$
$$-\frac{1}{4}$$

4.

$$\frac{7}{8}$$
$$-\frac{3}{7}$$

TEACHER NOTES: Subtracting Mixed Numbers
(Diagnostic Test Part II: Test Items 5–10)

Just as with adding and subtracting unlike denominators, the procedure is the same for adding and subtracting mixed numbers. In some cases, however, you must regroup a whole number into a fraction in order to subtract. Subtraction of mixed numbers should be taught at the same time as addition of mixed numbers.

TEACHING DEMONSTRATION

Use the following examples to demonstrate regrouping whole numbers into fractions. Ask students to regroup the mixed numbers below to show 1 less whole number.

Demonstrate regrouping.

$$3\frac{1}{8} = 2 + \frac{8}{8} + \frac{1}{8} = 2\frac{9}{8}$$

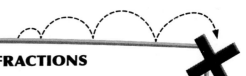

Ask students to regroup the following mixed numbers to show 1 less whole number.

1. $4 \dfrac{3}{4}$ = 3 + ___ + $\dfrac{3}{4}$ = 3 ___

2. $5 \dfrac{2}{3}$ = 4 + ___ + ___ = 4 ___

3. $2 \dfrac{6}{8}$ = ___ + $\dfrac{8}{8}$ + $\dfrac{6}{8}$ = ___ $\dfrac{14}{8}$

4. $1 \dfrac{5}{6}$ = ___ + ___ + ___ = _____

5. $7 \dfrac{7}{9}$ = ___ + ___ + ___ = _____

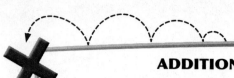
$$5 \frac{1}{4} - 2 \frac{5}{6}$$

Rewrite the problem in vertical form. Convert the fractions to equivalent fractions using the LCD of 12.

$$5 \frac{1}{4} = 5 \frac{3}{12}$$
$$- \ 2 \frac{5}{6} = 2 \frac{10}{12}$$

Because $\frac{3}{12} < \frac{10}{12}$, regroup $5 \frac{3}{12}$.

$$5 \frac{3}{12} = 4 + \frac{12}{12} + \frac{3}{12} = 4 \frac{15}{12}$$

Subtract the whole numbers. Then, subtract the fractions. Simplify if necessary.

$$4 \frac{15}{12}$$
$$- \ 2 \frac{10}{12}$$
$$2 \frac{5}{12}$$

Students need to practice several examples of subtraction with regrouping of a whole number into a fraction.

1.
$$6 \frac{1}{8}$$
$$- \ 4 \frac{3}{4}$$

2.
$$2 \frac{1}{3}$$
$$- \ 1 \frac{2}{5}$$

3.
$$4 \frac{1}{12}$$
$$- \ 2 \frac{3}{5}$$

4.
$$7 \frac{2}{7}$$
$$- \ 4 \frac{5}{6}$$

Subtracting Equivalent Fractions

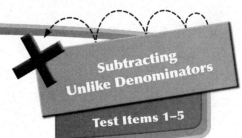

Subtracting
Unlike Denominators

Test Items 1–5

Directions: Study the example. Then, solve the subtraction problems. Write each difference in simplest form.

$$\frac{4}{6} = \frac{8}{12}$$

$$-\frac{1}{4} = \frac{3}{12}$$

$$\frac{5}{12}$$

Step 1: Find equivalent fractions by using the lowest common denominator.

Step 2: Subtract the numerators. Write the difference in simplest form.

1. $$\frac{3}{4}$$
$$-\frac{4}{6}$$

2. $$\frac{4}{5}$$
$$-\frac{7}{10}$$

3. $$\frac{2}{5}$$
$$-\frac{1}{9}$$

4. $$\frac{5}{6}$$
$$-\frac{2}{3}$$

5. $$\frac{2}{8}$$
$$-\frac{1}{12}$$

6. $$\frac{3}{4}$$
$$-\frac{1}{8}$$

7. $$\frac{5}{6}$$
$$-\frac{3}{9}$$

8. $$\frac{7}{12}$$
$$-\frac{1}{4}$$

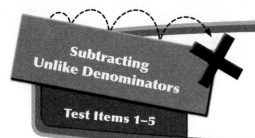

Steps to Subtraction

Directions: Solve the subtraction problems. Write each difference in simplest form.

1. $\dfrac{3}{4} - \dfrac{2}{8} =$

2. $\dfrac{4}{5} - \dfrac{1}{3} =$

3. $\dfrac{3}{5} - \dfrac{1}{2} =$

4. $\dfrac{4}{6} - \dfrac{1}{4} =$

5. $\dfrac{2}{3} - \dfrac{5}{9} =$

6. $\dfrac{5}{6} - \dfrac{1}{8} =$

7. $\dfrac{8}{9} - \dfrac{2}{3} =$

8. $\dfrac{5}{7} - \dfrac{1}{2} =$

9. $\dfrac{2}{4} - \dfrac{1}{2} =$

10. $\dfrac{5}{6} - \dfrac{2}{9} =$

Practice Makes Perfect

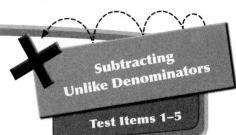

Subtracting Unlike Denominators

Test Items 1–5

Directions: Solve the subtraction problems. Write each answer in simplest form.

1. $\dfrac{7}{8} - \dfrac{1}{6} =$

2. $\begin{array}{r} \dfrac{9}{12} \\ -\ \dfrac{1}{2} \\ \hline \end{array}$

3. $\dfrac{8}{9} - \dfrac{3}{10} =$

4. $\begin{array}{r} \dfrac{5}{7} \\ -\ \dfrac{1}{2} \\ \hline \end{array}$

5. $\dfrac{6}{7} - \dfrac{1}{3} =$

6. $\begin{array}{r} \dfrac{5}{6} \\ -\ \dfrac{1}{4} \\ \hline \end{array}$

7. $\dfrac{4}{5} - \dfrac{1}{3} =$

8. $\begin{array}{r} \dfrac{6}{9} \\ -\ \dfrac{3}{6} \\ \hline \end{array}$

9. $\dfrac{1}{2} - \dfrac{2}{7} =$

NAME: _____ DATE: _____

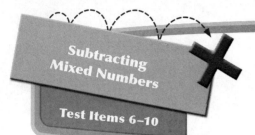

Subtracting Mixed Numbers

Test Items 6–10

Regrouping Mixed Numbers

Directions: Regroup the mixed numbers to show 1 less whole number. The first problem has been done for you.

1. $3 \frac{1}{8} = 2 + \frac{8}{8} + \frac{1}{8} = 2 \frac{9}{8}$

2. $4 \frac{3}{4} =$ _____

3. $5 \frac{1}{4} =$ _____

4. $2 \frac{5}{6} =$ _____

5. $2 \frac{2}{3} =$ _____

6. $4 \frac{1}{5} =$ _____

7. $1 \frac{6}{8} =$ _____

8. $3 \frac{4}{5} =$ _____

9. $4 \frac{7}{8} =$ _____

10. $6 \frac{1}{2} =$ _____

Fraction Subtraction

Directions: Study the example. Then, solve the subtraction problems. Regroup if needed. Write each difference in simplest form.

Example:

$$5 \frac{1}{4} = 5 \frac{3}{12} = 4 \frac{15}{12}$$
$$- 2 \frac{5}{6} = 2 \frac{10}{12} = 2 \frac{10}{12}$$
$$\overline{\qquad\qquad\qquad 2 \frac{5}{12}}$$

1.
$$3 \frac{1}{2}$$
$$- 2 \frac{5}{7}$$

2.
$$6 \frac{1}{2}$$
$$- 3 \frac{2}{3}$$

3.
$$3 \frac{4}{9}$$
$$- 1 \frac{1}{2}$$

4.
$$7 \frac{2}{4}$$
$$- 3 \frac{7}{8}$$

5.
$$2 \frac{1}{3}$$
$$- 1 \frac{5}{6}$$

6.
$$5 \frac{1}{4}$$
$$- 2 \frac{7}{8}$$

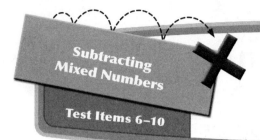

More
Fraction Subtraction

Directions: Solve the subtraction problems. Regroup if needed. Write each answer in simplest form.

1.
$$4 \tfrac{8}{12}$$
$$- \ 4 \tfrac{1}{2}$$

2.
$$8 \tfrac{3}{9}$$
$$- \ 3 \tfrac{5}{6}$$

3.
$$4 \tfrac{2}{4}$$
$$- \ 1 \tfrac{1}{2}$$

4.
$$4 \tfrac{3}{9}$$
$$- \ 4 \tfrac{1}{6}$$

5.
$$7 \tfrac{1}{2}$$
$$- \ 1 \tfrac{5}{7}$$

6.
$$4 \tfrac{1}{2}$$
$$- \ 2 \tfrac{7}{8}$$

7.
$$6 \tfrac{6}{7}$$
$$- \ 3 \tfrac{1}{2}$$

8.
$$8 \tfrac{2}{3}$$
$$- \ 5 \tfrac{11}{12}$$

9.
$$6 \tfrac{1}{2}$$
$$- \ 2 \tfrac{5}{6}$$

CD-104227 • Jump Into Math • © Carson-Dellosa

Diagnostic Test:
Multiplication and Division of Fractions

Directions: Write your answer to each question in the space provided. Write each answer in simplest form.

Part I: Multiplication

1. $\dfrac{1}{4}$ x 12 =

2. $\dfrac{1}{8}$ x 72 =

3. How much is $\dfrac{2}{3}$ of 10?

_____

4. How much is $\dfrac{8}{25}$ of 100 ?

_____

5. $\dfrac{7}{12}$ x $\dfrac{8}{21}$ =

6. $\dfrac{2}{3}$ x $\dfrac{3}{4}$ =

7. $\dfrac{2}{15}$ x $\dfrac{9}{8}$ =

8. 5 $\dfrac{2}{15}$ x 2 $\dfrac{9}{8}$ =

9. 3 x 7 $\dfrac{1}{8}$ =

10. 1 $\dfrac{5}{7}$ x 1 $\dfrac{5}{9}$ =

TEACHER ASSESSMENT AREA

Directions: Shade the boxes that correspond to correct test items.

Skill	Item Number			
Multiplying Whole Numbers by Fractions	1	2	3	4
Multiplying Fractions by Fractions	5	6	7	
Multiplying Mixed Numbers	8	9	10	

TOTAL CORRECT:_____

Teacher Notes and Activities

TEACHER NOTES: Multiplying Whole Numbers by Fractions
(Diagnostic Test Part I: Test Items 1–4)

There are several types of multiplication with fractions. Each type requires students to use a slightly different method. Most students find multiplication of fractions easier to solve than addition and subtraction of fractions. Multiplication does not require students to find common denominators before beginning the algorithm. Demonstrate the following examples for students before assigning individual practice.

TEACHING ACTIVITIES

"Multiplication as Repeated Addition" (Multiplying Whole Numbers by Fractions)

Multiplication of fractions can be solved as repeated addition, just as multiplication with whole numbers.

$$3 \times \frac{2}{7} = \frac{2}{7} + \frac{2}{7} + \frac{2}{7} = \frac{6}{7}$$

"Multiply the Numerator by the Whole Number"
(Multiplying Whole Numbers by Fractions)

To multiply a fraction by a whole number, multiply the numerator by the whole number. The denominator must remain the same since the whole number's assumed denominator is 1.

$$2 \times \frac{4}{9} = \frac{2}{1} \xrightarrow[\ (1 \times 9)\ ]{\ (2 \times 4)\ } \times \frac{4}{9} = \frac{8}{9}$$

$$5 \times \frac{3}{5} = \frac{5}{1} \xrightarrow[\ (1 \times 5)\ ]{\ (5 \times 3)\ } \times \frac{3}{5} = \frac{15}{5} = 3$$

$$8 \times \frac{2}{5} = \frac{8}{1} \xrightarrow[\ (1 \times 5)\ ]{\ (8 \times 2)\ } \times \frac{2}{5} = \frac{16}{5} = 3\frac{1}{5}$$

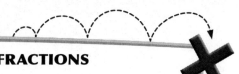

"Fractions That Divide" (Multiplying Whole Numbers by Fractions)

To multiply whole numbers by fractions, students should think, "take that fractional part of the whole number."
$\frac{1}{2}$ x 4 means one-half of 4, which is **2**. $\frac{1}{4}$ x 20 means one-fourth of 20, which is 5.
Although $\frac{1}{2}$ x 4 and $\frac{1}{4}$ x 20 are multiplication problems, they divide whole numbers by 2 and 4.

Explain to students that when a whole number is multiplied by a fraction with a numerator of 1, they can divide the whole number by the denominator. Demonstrate with the examples below.

$$\frac{1}{2} \text{ x } 4$$

$\frac{1}{2}$ x 4 is also one-half of 4, or 4 ÷ 2.

$$\frac{1}{2} \text{ x } 4 = 4 \div 2 = 2$$

$$\frac{1}{4} \text{ x } 20$$

$\frac{1}{4}$ x 20 is also one-fourth of 20, or 20 ÷ 4.

$$\frac{1}{4} \text{ x } 20 = 20 \div 4 = 5$$

$$\frac{1}{3} \text{ x } 21$$

$\frac{1}{3}$ x 21 is also one-third of 21, or 21 ÷ 3.

$$\frac{1}{3} \text{ x } 21 = 21 \div 3 = 7$$

TEACHER NOTES: Multiplying Fractions by Fractions
(Diagnostic Test Part I: Test Items 5–7)

Multiplying a fraction by a fraction is much easier if both fractions are in simplest form. Students simply multiply the numerators and the denominators, then check to see that the product is in simplest form.

$$\frac{2}{3} \times \frac{3}{4} = \frac{2 \times 3}{3 \times 4} = \frac{6}{12} = \frac{1}{2}$$

TEACHING ACTIVITY: "The Cancellation Rule"
(Multiplying Fractions by Fractions)

Demonstrate for students how to solve problems in a different way using the cancellation rule. This rule allows students to divide opposite numerators and denominators by a common factor. The cancellation rule simplifies fractions before multiplication, making the algorithm easier and generating products in simplest form.

$$\frac{2}{3} \times \frac{3}{4}$$

Step 1: The first denominator and second numerator have a common factor of 3. Divide both by 3.

$$\frac{2}{\cancel{3}} \times \frac{\cancel{3}^{1}}{4} = \frac{2 \times \cancel{3}^{1}}{\cancel{3}_{1} \times 4}$$

Step 2: The first numerator and second denominator also have a common factor of 2. Divide both by 2.

$$\frac{\cancel{2}}{3} \times \frac{3}{\cancel{4}} = \frac{\cancel{2}^{1} \times \cancel{3}^{1}}{\cancel{3}_{1} \times \cancel{4}_{2}}$$

Step 3: Multiply the new factors. The product is already in simplest form!

$$\frac{2}{3} \times \frac{3}{4} = \frac{\cancel{2}^{1} \times \cancel{3}^{1}}{\cancel{3}_{1} \times \cancel{4}_{2}} = \frac{1 \times 1}{1 \times 2} = \frac{1}{2}$$

$$\frac{8}{9} \times \frac{15}{16}$$

- 8 and 16 have a common factor of 8. Divide both by 8.
- 9 and 15 have a common factor of 3. Divide both by 3.
- Multiply the new factors.

$$\frac{\cancel{8}^{1}}{\cancel{9}_{3}} \times \frac{\cancel{15}^{5}}{\cancel{16}_{2}} = \frac{1 \times 5}{3 \times 2} = \frac{5}{6}$$

$$\frac{8}{9} \times \frac{15}{16} = \frac{5}{6}$$

CD-104227 • Jump Into Math • © Carson-Dellosa

TEACHER NOTES: Multiplying Mixed Numbers

(Diagnostic Test Part I: Test Items 8–10)

When multiplying two mixed numbers, students must first change the mixed numbers to improper fractions.

TEACHING ACTIVITIES

"Making Fractions Improper" (Multiplying Mixed Numbers)

Let students practice changing mixed numbers to improper fractions before modeling the example below.

$$1\frac{3}{5} \times 3\frac{1}{2}$$

Step 1: Change each mixed fraction to an improper fraction. To do so, multiply the denominator by the whole number and add to the numerator.

$$1\frac{3}{5} = \frac{8}{5} \quad (5 \times 1 + 3)$$

$$3\frac{1}{2} = \frac{7}{2} \quad (2 \times 3 + 1)$$

Step 2: Use the cancellation rule to simplify. 8 and 2 have a common factor of 2. Divide both by 2.

$$\frac{\cancel{8}^{4}}{5} \times \frac{7}{\cancel{2}_{1}}$$

Step 3: Multiply the new factors. Then, change the product into a mixed number.

$$\frac{8}{5} \times \frac{7}{2} = \frac{4 \times 7}{5 \times 1} = \frac{28}{5} = 5\frac{3}{5}$$

"Multiply a Whole Number by a Mixed Number"

When multiplying by a whole number, it is not necessary to change mixed numbers to improper fractions. Multiply the whole number by the mixed fraction's whole number, then multiply the whole number by the numerator of the fraction.

$$2 \times 4\frac{1}{3}$$

Step 1: Multiply the whole numbers. $2 \times 4 = 8$

Step 2: Multiply the whole number by the fraction. Then, add the results.

$$2 \times \frac{1}{3} = \frac{2}{3} \qquad\qquad 8 + \frac{2}{3} = 8\frac{2}{3}$$

Follow the Rule

Directions: Study the rule below. Then, solve the multiplication problems.

Rule: To multiply a fraction by a whole number, multiply the numerator by the whole number. Keep the same denominator. Simplify the product if needed.

$$4 \times \frac{3}{5} = \frac{12}{5} = 2\frac{2}{5}$$

1. $6 \times \dfrac{2}{3} =$

2. $7 \times \dfrac{3}{5} =$

3. $4 \times \dfrac{1}{2} =$

4. $9 \times \dfrac{7}{8} =$

5. $10 \times \dfrac{4}{5} =$

6. $3 \times \dfrac{2}{7} =$

7. $4 \times \dfrac{2}{9} =$

8. $5 \times \dfrac{3}{8} =$

9. $3 \times \dfrac{3}{10} =$

10. $7 \times \dfrac{2}{3} =$

NAME: _____   DATE: _____

Multiplication as Fractional Parts

Directions: Study the rule below. Then, rewrite each problem in words. Finally, multiply.

Rule: To multiply a fraction by a whole number, find that fractional part of the whole number. Multiply the numerator of the fraction by the whole number. The denominator stays the same since you multiply it by 1. Simplify the fraction to find the new number.

$\dfrac{1}{2}$ x 4 means one-half of 4 $\dfrac{1}{2}$ x $\dfrac{4}{1}$ = $\dfrac{4}{2}$ = 2

1. $\dfrac{3}{4}$ x 20 means _____three-fourths of 20_____ $\dfrac{3}{4}$ x $\dfrac{20}{1}$ = $\dfrac{60}{4}$ = 15

2. $\dfrac{5}{9}$ x 9 means _____ $\dfrac{5}{9}$ x $\dfrac{9}{1}$ =

3. $\dfrac{1}{5}$ x 25 means _____ $\dfrac{1}{5}$ x $\dfrac{25}{1}$ =

4. $\dfrac{3}{4}$ x 100 means _____ $\dfrac{3}{4}$ x $\dfrac{100}{1}$ =

5. $\dfrac{7}{10}$ x 100 means _____ $\dfrac{7}{10}$ x $\dfrac{100}{1}$ =

6. $\dfrac{2}{5}$ x 40 means _____ $\dfrac{2}{5}$ x $\dfrac{100}{1}$ =

7. $\dfrac{1}{3}$ x 18 means _____ $\dfrac{1}{3}$ x $\dfrac{18}{1}$ =

NAME: _____ DATE: _____

Cancel and Multiply

Directions: Study the rule below. Then, cancel and multiply.

The **Cancellation Rule** allows you to divide opposite numerators and denominators by a common factor before you multiply.

$$\frac{1}{3} \times 9 = \frac{1}{\cancel{3}_{1}} \times \frac{\cancel{9}^{3}}{1} = \frac{1 \times 3}{1 \times 1} = 3$$

1. $\frac{2}{3} \times 12 =$

2. $\frac{4}{5} \times 20 =$

3. $18 \times \frac{1}{6} =$

4. $27 \times \frac{5}{9} =$

5. $36 \times \frac{5}{6} =$

6. $\frac{3}{4} \times 24 =$

7. $\frac{1}{2} \times 14 =$

8. $40 \times \frac{5}{8} =$

9. $21 \times \frac{2}{3} =$

10. $24 \times \frac{2}{3} =$

CD-104227 • Jump Into Math • © Carson-Dellosa

Multiplying Fractions Is Easy!

Multiplying
Fractions by Fractions

Test Items 5–7

Directions: Look at the example. Then, solve the multiplication problems.

If both factors are in simplest form, multiplication of fractions is easy. Multiply the numerators. Then, multiply the denominators. Write your answer in simplest form.

$$\frac{2}{3} \times \frac{3}{4} = \frac{2 \times 3}{3 \times 4} = \frac{6}{12} = \frac{1}{2}$$

1. $\frac{2}{5} \times \frac{3}{5} =$ 2. $\frac{2}{3} \times \frac{5}{6} =$ 3. $\frac{2}{5} \times \frac{1}{4} =$

4. $\frac{2}{9} \times \frac{3}{8} =$ 5. $\frac{1}{4} \times \frac{3}{5} =$ 6. $\frac{1}{3} \times \frac{2}{7} =$

7. $\frac{3}{4} \times \frac{4}{5} =$ 8. $\frac{2}{7} \times \frac{5}{6} =$ 9. $\frac{1}{3} \times \frac{7}{8} =$

10. $\frac{3}{4} \times \frac{5}{9} =$ 11. $\frac{5}{6} \times \frac{3}{7} =$ 12. $\frac{5}{9} \times \frac{2}{3} =$

Use the Cancellation Rule

Directions: Use the cancellation rule to simplify the fractions. Then, multiply.

Cancellation Rule: Divide opposite numerators and denominators by common factors. Then, multiply. In the example below, the 3s share a factor of 3. The 2 and 4 share a factor of 2.

$$\frac{2}{3} \times \frac{3}{4} = \frac{\cancel{2} \times \cancel{3}}{\cancel{3} \times \cancel{4}} = \frac{1 \times 1}{1 \times 2} = \frac{1}{2}$$

1. $\dfrac{8}{9} \times \dfrac{15}{16} =$

2. $\dfrac{7}{12} \times \dfrac{8}{21} =$

3. $\dfrac{2}{15} \times \dfrac{9}{8} =$

4. $\dfrac{9}{10} \times \dfrac{25}{33} =$

5. $\dfrac{3}{8} \times \dfrac{4}{9} =$

6. $\dfrac{6}{35} \times \dfrac{20}{24} =$

7. $\dfrac{4}{9} \times \dfrac{9}{4} =$

8. $\dfrac{3}{7} \times \dfrac{14}{15} =$

9. $\dfrac{2}{9} \times \dfrac{18}{20} =$

10. $\dfrac{4}{5} \times \dfrac{10}{12} =$

NAME: _____ DATE: _____

Mixed Fraction Multiplication Practice

Directions: Solve the multiplication problems. Use the cancellation rule when possible. Write each answer in simplest form.

1. $12 \times \dfrac{5}{8} =$

2. $42 \times \dfrac{3}{7} =$

3. $\dfrac{3}{4} \times \dfrac{16}{24} =$

4. $12 \times \dfrac{7}{9} =$

5. $\dfrac{4}{5} \times \dfrac{25}{28} =$

6. $\dfrac{2}{3} \times \dfrac{15}{18} =$

7. $\dfrac{6}{7} \times \dfrac{24}{36} =$

8. $18 \times \dfrac{4}{9} =$

9. $\dfrac{18}{25} \times \dfrac{20}{27} =$

10. $\dfrac{24}{30} \times \dfrac{18}{36} =$

NAME: _____ DATE: _____

Multiplying
Mixed Numbers

Test Items 8–10

Multiplying Mixed Numbers

Directions: Study the example below. Then, solve the multiplication problems. Write each answer in simplest form.

Example:

Step 1: Change both mixed fractions to improper fractions.

$$1\frac{3}{5} \times 3\frac{1}{2} = \frac{8}{5} \times \frac{7}{2}$$

Step 2: Use the cancellation rule if possible.

$$\frac{\overset{4}{\cancel{8}} \times 7}{5 \times \underset{1}{\cancel{2}}}$$

Step 3: Multiply.

$$\frac{4}{5} \times \frac{7}{1} = \frac{28}{5}$$

Step 4: Simplify.

$$\frac{28}{5} = 5\frac{3}{5}$$

1. $1\frac{1}{5} \times 6\frac{7}{8} =$

2. $2\frac{2}{5} \times 8\frac{1}{2} =$

3. $\frac{5}{6} \times 2\frac{1}{10} =$

4. $6\frac{3}{4} \times 4\frac{1}{2} =$

5. $4\frac{2}{5} \times \frac{5}{11} =$

6. $3\frac{1}{8} \times 2\frac{2}{3} =$

7. $4\frac{1}{2} \times 2\frac{1}{3} =$

8. $5\frac{3}{4} \times 2\frac{1}{3} =$

118

CD-104227 • Jump Into Math • © Carson-Dellosa

Multiplying Whole Numbers by Mixed Numbers

Directions: Study the examples below. Then, solve the multiplication problems. Write your answers in simplest form.

When multiplying a mixed number by a whole number, multiply the whole numbers first. Then, multiply the whole number by the fraction. Add the products and simplify.

Examples: $3 \times 4\frac{2}{3} = 12 + (3 \times \frac{2}{3}) = 12 + \frac{6}{3} = 12 + 2 = 14$

$2 \times 4\frac{1}{3} = 8 + (2 \times \frac{1}{3}) = 8 + \frac{2}{3} = 8\frac{2}{3}$

1. $3 \times 2\frac{2}{3} =$

2. $4 \times 1\frac{7}{8} =$

3. $5 \times 3\frac{5}{6} =$

4. $8 \times 4\frac{1}{3} =$

5. $7 \times 3\frac{2}{5} =$

6. $2 \times 3\frac{3}{4} =$

7. $5 \times 4\frac{6}{7} =$

8. $7 \times 3\frac{7}{9} =$

Mixed Numbers Multiplication Practice

Directions: Solve the multiplication problems. Write your answers in simplest form.

1. $2 \dfrac{1}{2} \times 3 \dfrac{2}{3} =$

2. $4 \times 3 \dfrac{1}{8} =$

3. $8 \times 2 \dfrac{3}{4} =$

4. $4 \dfrac{3}{4} \times 2 \dfrac{7}{8} =$

5. $4 \dfrac{5}{8} \times 3 \dfrac{1}{4} =$

6. $4 \dfrac{2}{3} \times 2 \dfrac{5}{6} =$

7. $12 \times 3 \dfrac{3}{4} =$

8. $5 \dfrac{1}{3} \times 2 \dfrac{2}{9} =$

9. $6 \dfrac{2}{3} \times 3 \dfrac{1}{2} =$

10. $18 \times 2 \dfrac{4}{9} =$

NAME: _____ DATE: _____

Diagnostic Test:
Multiplication and Division of Fractions

Directions: Write your answer to each question in the space provided. Write each answer in simplest form. Use another sheet of paper to show your work if necessary.

Part II: Division

1. $2 \div \dfrac{1}{5} =$

2. $3 \div \dfrac{1}{4} =$

3. $\dfrac{2}{3} \div 4 =$

4. $\dfrac{3}{4} \div \dfrac{1}{2} =$

5. $\dfrac{1}{4} \div \dfrac{2}{3} =$

6. $\dfrac{5}{6} \div \dfrac{8}{9} =$

7. $\dfrac{3}{7} \div \dfrac{6}{7} =$

8. $2\dfrac{1}{2} \div 1\dfrac{1}{4} =$

9. $2\dfrac{5}{6} \div 1\dfrac{1}{2} =$

10. $4\dfrac{2}{3} \div \dfrac{3}{4} =$

TEACHER ASSESSMENT AREA

Directions: Shade the boxes that correspond to correct test items.

Skill	Item Number			
Dividing Whole Numbers and Fractions	1	2	3	
Dividing Fractions by Fractions	4	5	6	7
Dividing Mixed Numbers	8	9	10	

TOTAL CORRECT: _____

Teacher Notes and Activities

TEACHER NOTES: Division of Fractions

(Diagnostic Test Part II: Test Items 1–10)

One of the most difficult operations for students to understand is division of fractions. Begin by reviewing the relationship between multiplication and division. These operations are opposite, or inverse, operations.

Two methods are commonly used to divide fractions. One is the common denominator method, and the other is the reciprocal method.

TEACHING ACTIVITIES

"Common Denominator Method" (Division of Fractions)

Introduce the division of fractions with whole numbers. This will help students see the process and check their initial work. Begin with a basic fact, such as $15 \div 5$. Then, convert the numbers to fractions.

$$15 \div 5 = \frac{15}{1} \div \frac{5}{1} = \frac{3}{1} = 3$$

Move on to pairs of fractions with the same denominator. Explain to students that to divide fractions with the same denominator, they only need to divide the numerators. Demonstrate with the problem below.

$$\frac{14}{20} \div \frac{15}{20} = \frac{14 \div 15}{20 \div 20} = \frac{14 \div 15}{1} = \frac{14}{15}$$

Remind students that expressions in the form $a \div b$ are the same as $\frac{a}{b}$. So, $14 \div 15$ is the same as $\frac{14}{15}$.

Explain to students that to divide fractions with different denominators, they must change the fractions to equivalent fractions with a common denominator. Then, they can divide and simplify their answers.

$$\frac{2}{5} \div \frac{3}{4} = \frac{8}{20} \div \frac{15}{20} = \frac{8 \div 15}{1} = \frac{8}{15}$$

$$\frac{3}{5} \div \frac{2}{3} = \frac{9}{15} \div \frac{10}{15} = \frac{9 \div 10}{1} = \frac{9}{10}$$

To divide a whole number by a fraction or a fraction by a whole number, students must write the whole number as a fraction. Then, they must find a common denominator and divide.

$$3 \div \frac{1}{4} = \frac{3}{1} \div \frac{1}{4} = \frac{12}{4} \div \frac{1}{4} = \frac{12 \div 1}{1} = \frac{12}{1} = 12$$

$$\frac{2}{3} \div 5 = \frac{2}{3} \div \frac{5}{1} = \frac{2}{3} \div \frac{15}{3} = \frac{2 \div 15}{1} = \frac{2}{15}$$

To divide mixed numbers, students must convert the mixed numbers to improper fractions. Then, they must find a common denominator and divide.

$$3\frac{1}{2} \div 2\frac{1}{4} = \frac{7}{2} \div \frac{9}{4} = \frac{14}{4} \div \frac{9}{4} = \frac{14 \div 9}{4 \div 4} = \frac{14 \div 9}{1} = \frac{14}{9} = 1\frac{5}{9}$$

"Reciprocal Method" (Division of Fractions)

Explain to students that reciprocals are two numbers whose product is 1. For example, $\frac{1}{8}$ is the reciprocal of 8, which can be represented as $\frac{8}{1}$. Instruct students to find the reciprocal of each number below.

The reciprocal of $\frac{1}{4}$ is _____.

The reciprocal of $\frac{5}{6}$ is _____.

The reciprocal of 3 is _____.

The reciprocal of 7 is _____.

Explain to students that to find the reciprocal of a mixed number, they must first convert the number to an improper fraction. Then, they can invert the numerator and denominator.

$$1\frac{2}{3} = \frac{5}{3}, \text{ so the reciprocal is: } \frac{3}{5}. \qquad 2\frac{3}{5} = \frac{13}{5}, \text{ so the reciprocal is: } \frac{5}{13}.$$

$$3\frac{1}{4} = \frac{13}{4}, \text{ so the reciprocal is: \_\_\_\_}. \qquad 2\frac{7}{8} = \frac{23}{8}, \text{ so the reciprocal is: \_\_\_\_}.$$

To divide a whole number by a fraction or a fraction by a whole number, students must multiply by the reciprocal of the divisor.

$$2 \div \frac{1}{3} = 2 \times \frac{3}{1} = 6$$

$$\frac{1}{3} \div 2 = \frac{1}{3} \times \frac{1}{2} = \frac{1}{6}$$

To divide a fraction by a fraction, students must multiply the dividend by the reciprocal of the divisor.

$$\frac{4}{9} \div \frac{2}{3} = \frac{4}{9} \times \frac{3}{2} = \frac{12}{18} = \frac{2}{3}$$

To divide mixed numbers, students must first convert the mixed numbers to improper fractions.

$$3\frac{1}{2} \div 2\frac{1}{4} = \frac{7}{2} \div \frac{9}{4}$$

Then, they must multiply the dividend by the reciprocal of the divisor.

$$\frac{7}{2} \div \frac{9}{4} = \frac{7}{2} \times \frac{4}{9} = \frac{28}{18} = 1\frac{10}{18} = 1\frac{5}{9}$$

Using Reciprocals

Directions: Practice writing the reciprocals of fractions. Then, use reciprocals to solve the division problems. Write your answers in simplest form.

To divide a whole number by a fraction, multiply the dividend by the **reciprocal** of the divisor. Remember, reciprocals are two numbers that, when multiplied together, have a product of 1.

Example: The reciprocal of $\frac{1}{3}$ is 3 because $\frac{1}{3}$ x $\frac{3}{3}$ = $\frac{3}{3}$ = 1.

$$2 \div \frac{1}{3} = 2 \times \frac{3}{1} = 6$$

1. The reciprocal of $\frac{1}{4}$ is _____.

2. The reciprocal of $\frac{3}{4}$ is _____.

3. The reciprocal of $\frac{5}{6}$ is _____.

4. The reciprocal of $\frac{2}{3}$ is _____.

5. The reciprocal of $\frac{1}{5}$ is _____.

6. The reciprocal of $\frac{5}{7}$ is _____.

7. The reciprocal of $\frac{2}{9}$ is _____.

8. The reciprocal of $\frac{4}{5}$ is _____.

9. The reciprocal of $\frac{1}{6}$ is _____.

10. The reciprocal of $\frac{3}{7}$ is _____.

11. $2 \div \frac{2}{3} =$

12. $5 \div \frac{1}{5} =$

13. $6 \div \frac{3}{4} =$

14. $7 \div \frac{5}{6} =$

15. $10 \div \frac{5}{7} =$

16. $4 \div \frac{2}{9} =$

17. $9 \div \frac{4}{5} =$

18. $11 \div \frac{1}{6} =$

19. $3 \div \frac{3}{7} =$

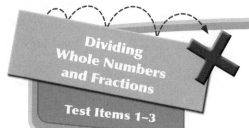

Divide with Reciprocals

Directions: Practice writing the reciprocals of fractions. Then, use reciprocals to solve the division problems. Write each answer in simplest form.

To divide a fraction by a whole number, multiply the dividend by the **reciprocal** of the divisor.

Example: The reciprocal of 8 is $\dfrac{1}{8}$ because $\dfrac{8}{1}$ x $\dfrac{1}{8}$ = $\dfrac{8}{8}$ = 1 .

$$\dfrac{1}{4} \div 8 = \dfrac{1}{4} \times \dfrac{1}{8} = \dfrac{1}{32}$$

1. The reciprocal of 4 is _____ .

2. The reciprocal of 7 is _____ .

3. The reciprocal of 9 is _____ .

4. The reciprocal of 2 is _____ .

5. The reciprocal of 3 is _____ .

6. The reciprocal of 11 is_____ .

7. The reciprocal of 24 is _____ .

8. The reciprocal of 6 is _____ .

9. The reciprocal of 15 is _____ .

10. The reciprocal of 5 is _____ .

11. $\dfrac{2}{3} \div 7 =$

12. $\dfrac{1}{4} \div 4 =$

13. $\dfrac{2}{3} \div 3 =$

14. $\dfrac{4}{5} \div 2 =$

15. $\dfrac{3}{4} \div 9 =$

16. $\dfrac{5}{6} \div 6 =$

17. $\dfrac{2}{7} \div 5 =$

18. $\dfrac{1}{8} \div 11 =$

19. $\dfrac{3}{5} \div 24 =$

 CD-104227 • Jump Into Math • © Carson-Dellosa

Practice with Reciprocals

Dividing
Whole Numbers
and Fractions

Test Items 1–3

Directions: Write the reciprocal of each number below. Then, solve the division problems. Write each answer in simplest form.

1. The reciprocal of $\frac{1}{2}$ is _____.

2. The reciprocal of 4 is _____.

3. The reciprocal of 6 is _____.

4. The reciprocal of $\frac{2}{3}$ is _____.

5. The reciprocal of $\frac{3}{4}$ is _____.

6. The reciprocal of $\frac{1}{8}$ is _____.

7. The reciprocal of 9 is _____.

8. The reciprocal of $\frac{5}{7}$ is _____.

9. The reciprocal of $\frac{8}{9}$ is _____.

10. The reciprocal of 8 is _____.

11. $3 \div \frac{2}{3} =$

12. $\frac{3}{4} \div 7 =$

13. $4 \div \frac{8}{9} =$

14. $\frac{5}{7} \div 6 =$

15. $8 \div \frac{1}{8} =$

16. $11 \div \frac{7}{9} =$

17. $\frac{1}{2} \div 9 =$

18. $10 \div \frac{4}{5} =$

19. $\frac{5}{7} \div 3 =$

Common Denominator Method

Directions: Use the common denominator method to solve the division problems. Write each answer in simplest form.

When dividing fractions with different denominators, change the fractions to equivalent fractions with a common denominator. Then, divide and write the quotient in simplest form.

Remember: $a \div b = \dfrac{a}{b}$.

$$\frac{2}{5} \div \frac{3}{4} = \frac{8}{20} \div \frac{15}{20} = \frac{8 \div 15}{1} = \frac{8}{15}$$

1. $\dfrac{5}{7} \div \dfrac{1}{3} =$

2. $\dfrac{1}{3} \div \dfrac{3}{6} =$

3. $\dfrac{4}{12} \div \dfrac{3}{4} =$

4. $\dfrac{2}{5} \div \dfrac{1}{2} =$

5. $\dfrac{11}{18} \div \dfrac{1}{3} =$

6. $\dfrac{1}{6} \div \dfrac{1}{3} =$

7. $\dfrac{1}{3} \div \dfrac{4}{5} =$

8. $\dfrac{1}{4} \div \dfrac{4}{8} =$

9. $\dfrac{1}{2} \div \dfrac{5}{8} =$

10. $\dfrac{4}{12} \div \dfrac{1}{2} =$

CD-104227 • Jump Into Math • © Carson-Dellosa

NAME: _____   DATE: _____

Reciprocal Method

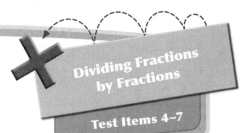

Dividing Fractions
by Fractions

Test Items 4–7

Directions: Use the reciprocal method to solve the division problems. Be sure to use the cancellation rule if possible. Write each answer in simplest form.

To divide a fraction by a fraction, multiply the dividend by the reciprocal of the divisor.

$$\frac{4}{9} \div \frac{2}{3} = \frac{4}{9} \times \frac{3}{2} = \frac{12}{18} = \frac{2}{3}$$

Use the cancellation rule if possible:

$$\frac{4}{3} \div \frac{2}{9} = \frac{\overset{2}{\cancel{4}}}{\underset{1}{\cancel{3}}} \times \frac{\overset{3}{\cancel{9}}}{\underset{1}{\cancel{2}}} = \frac{2 \times 3}{1 \times 1} = 6$$

Your answer will already be in simplest form!

1. $\frac{3}{4} \div \frac{1}{9} =$

2. $\frac{7}{8} \div \frac{4}{5} =$

3. $\frac{3}{16} \div \frac{9}{10} =$

4. $\frac{4}{16} \div \frac{1}{6} =$

5. $\frac{2}{6} \div \frac{12}{14} =$

6. $\frac{6}{15} \div \frac{1}{2} =$

7. $\frac{2}{3} \div \frac{6}{9} =$

8. $\frac{8}{12} \div \frac{12}{14} =$

9. $\frac{2}{9} \div \frac{6}{7} =$

10. $\frac{9}{10} \div \frac{6}{7} =$

Dividing Fractions by Fractions

Test Items 4–7

Choose a Method

Directions: Solve the division problems. Write each answer in simplest form.

COMMON DENOMINATOR METHOD

$$\frac{1}{2} \div \frac{5}{6} = \frac{3}{6} \div \frac{5}{6} = \frac{3 \div 5}{1} = \frac{3}{5}$$

RECIPROCAL METHOD WITH CANCELLATION RULE

$$\frac{1}{2} \div \frac{5}{6} = \frac{1}{\overset{}{\underset{1}{\cancel{2}}}} \times \frac{\overset{3}{\cancel{6}}}{5} = \frac{3}{5}$$

---

1. $\dfrac{3}{4} \div \dfrac{4}{5} =$

2. $\dfrac{3}{5} \div \dfrac{2}{3} =$

3. $\dfrac{2}{9} \div \dfrac{4}{18} =$

4. $\dfrac{4}{5} \div \dfrac{3}{15} =$

5. $\dfrac{5}{6} \div \dfrac{8}{9} =$

6. $\dfrac{4}{15} \div \dfrac{9}{10} =$

7. $\dfrac{5}{8} \div \dfrac{11}{12} =$

8. $\dfrac{3}{4} \div \dfrac{1}{2} =$

9. $\dfrac{1}{3} \div \dfrac{1}{6} =$

10. $\dfrac{5}{8} \div \dfrac{4}{5} =$

NAME: _____   DATE: _____

Convert to Divide

Dividing Mixed Numbers

Test Items 8–10

Directions: Rewrite each number as an improper fraction.

To divide mixed numbers, first convert them to improper fractions. Then, multiply the dividend by the reciprocal of the divisor. Simplify the quotient.

$$2\frac{1}{4} \div 1\frac{1}{3} = \frac{9}{4} \div \frac{4}{3} = \frac{9}{4} \times \frac{3}{4} = \frac{27}{16} = 1\frac{11}{16}$$

1. $1\frac{5}{9} =$

2. $2\frac{3}{4} =$

3. $4\frac{1}{2} =$

4. $3\frac{1}{3} =$

5. $2\frac{7}{8} =$

6. $6\frac{1}{10} =$

7. $1\frac{4}{16} =$

8. $4\frac{2}{3} =$

Directions: Convert the mixed numbers to improper fractions. Then, divide using the reciprocal method. Write each answer in simplest form.

9. $2\frac{2}{5} \div 8\frac{1}{2} =$

10. $6\frac{4}{8} \div 1\frac{5}{9} =$

11. $\frac{5}{7} \div 1\frac{3}{5} =$

12. $2\frac{7}{18} \div \frac{1}{3} =$

13. $5\frac{6}{7} \div 3\frac{14}{15} =$

14. $\frac{13}{15} \div 2\frac{6}{7} =$

15. $1\frac{4}{7} \div \frac{3}{4} =$

16. $6\frac{1}{2} \div 2\frac{1}{3} =$

17. $4\frac{1}{2} \div 5\frac{3}{6} =$

18. $3\frac{1}{3} \div \frac{3}{4} =$

Match Them Up!

Directions: Match each mixed number division problem in the left column with its reciprocal method problem in the right column. In the reciprocal method problems, the mixed numbers have been converted to improper fractions and the divisors are written as reciprocals.

1. $\dfrac{2}{5} \div 1\dfrac{5}{6} =$

2. $2\dfrac{3}{10} \div 2\dfrac{5}{13} =$

3. $5\dfrac{6}{7} \div 3\dfrac{14}{15} =$

4. $2\dfrac{2}{3} \div \dfrac{4}{9} =$

5. $7\dfrac{6}{7} \div 5\dfrac{8}{10} =$

6. $3\dfrac{3}{7} \div 5 =$

7. $2\dfrac{3}{4} \div 4\dfrac{1}{3} =$

8. $1\dfrac{3}{8} \div 4\dfrac{5}{7} =$

9. $9\dfrac{2}{3} \div 3\dfrac{1}{6} =$

10. $2\dfrac{5}{6} \div 2\dfrac{2}{9} =$

11. $6\dfrac{1}{4} \div 3\dfrac{2}{5} =$

12. $7\dfrac{2}{3} \div \dfrac{6}{7} =$

A. $\dfrac{55}{7} \times \dfrac{10}{58} =$

B. $\dfrac{23}{10} \times \dfrac{13}{31} =$

C. $\dfrac{11}{4} \times \dfrac{3}{13} =$

D. $\dfrac{29}{3} \times \dfrac{6}{19} =$

E. $\dfrac{2}{5} \times \dfrac{6}{11} =$

F. $\dfrac{17}{6} \times \dfrac{9}{20} =$

G. $\dfrac{25}{4} \times \dfrac{5}{17} =$

H. $\dfrac{41}{7} \times \dfrac{15}{59} =$

I. $\dfrac{24}{7} \times \dfrac{1}{5} =$

J. $\dfrac{23}{3} \times \dfrac{7}{6} =$

K. $\dfrac{8}{3} \times \dfrac{9}{4} =$

L. $\dfrac{11}{8} \times \dfrac{7}{33} =$

CD-104227 • Jump Into Math • © Carson-Dellosa

Mixed Practice

Division of Fractions

Test Items 1–10

Directions: Solve the division problems. Work on one column at a time. Show your work on a separate sheet of paper. Write each answer in simplest form.

Column A

1. $\dfrac{2}{3} \div \dfrac{1}{2} =$

2. $8 \div \dfrac{3}{4} =$

3. $\dfrac{7}{8} \div 12 =$

4. $\dfrac{5}{7} \div 1\dfrac{3}{5} =$

5. $2\dfrac{2}{3} \div \dfrac{4}{9} =$

6. $3\dfrac{3}{7} \div 5 =$

7. $2\dfrac{3}{4} \div 4\dfrac{1}{3} =$

8. $\dfrac{5}{7} \div \dfrac{1}{2} =$

Column B

1. $6 \div 3\dfrac{1}{3} =$

2. $\dfrac{1}{6} \div \dfrac{1}{3} =$

3. $2 \div \dfrac{2}{3} =$

4. $1\dfrac{3}{8} \div 4\dfrac{5}{7} =$

5. $\dfrac{1}{2} \div \dfrac{5}{8} =$

6. $9 \div \dfrac{4}{5} =$

7. $9\dfrac{2}{3} \div 3\dfrac{1}{6} =$

8. $\dfrac{3}{4} \div \dfrac{1}{9} =$

Column C

1. $11 \div \dfrac{7}{9} =$

2. $6\dfrac{1}{4} \div 3\dfrac{2}{5} =$

3. $\dfrac{4}{5} \div 2 =$

4. $\dfrac{4}{16} \div \dfrac{1}{6} =$

5. $\dfrac{3}{4} \div \dfrac{2}{3} =$

6. $7\dfrac{2}{3} \div \dfrac{6}{7} =$

7. $\dfrac{2}{3} \div 6 =$

8. $\dfrac{7}{8} \div 2\dfrac{5}{6} =$

Diagnostic Test: Number Theory

Directions: Write your answer to each question in the space provided.

1. Circle the number that is divisible by 9.

   548   236   325   5,445

2. Circle the number that is divisible by 6.

   304   366   446   2666

3. Circle your answer.
   31 is a _____ number.
   prime   composite

4. Circle your answer.
   78 is a _____ number.
   prime   composite

5. Write 3 x 3 x 3 x 3 in exponential form.

   _____

6. Write 10^3 in factor form.

   _____

7. Write 2^5 in standard form.

   _____

8. List the prime factors of 36.

   _____

9. Multiply the prime factors to name the number.

   2 x 2 x 2 x 3 x 5

   _____

10. List the prime factors of 70.

   _____

TEACHER ASSESSMENT AREA

Directions: Shade the boxes that correspond to correct test items.

TOTAL CORRECT: _____

Skill	Item Number		
Divisibility Rules	1	2	
Prime and Composite Numbers	3	4	
Exponents	5	6	7
Prime Factorization	8	9	10

CD-104227 • Jump Into Math • © Carson-Dellosa

Teacher Notes and Activities

BACKGROUND INFORMATION

Number theory at the fifth-grade level sets the stage for algebra. Divisibility rules, prime and composite numbers, exponents, and prime factorization form the foundation for later success in algebra.

TEACHER NOTES: Divisibility Rules

(Diagnostic Test Part I: Test Items 1–2)

A whole number is "divisible" by another whole number when the remainder is 0 after division. There are rules that students can follow to determine divisibility by a number from 2–10 without dividing. Present the following math "tricks" or divisibility rules and examples to your students. Make copies of the chart for students to use as a reference with the student worksheet on page 142.

TEACHING ACTIVITY: "Divisibility Tricks" (Divisibility Rules)

DIVISIBILITY RULES	EXAMPLES
A number is divisible by 2 if the last digit is 0, 2, 4, 6, or 8.	168 is divisible by 2, since the last digit is 8.
A number is divisible by 3 if the sum of the digits is divisible by 3.	168 is divisible by 3, since the sum of the digits is 15 (1 + 6 + 8 = 15). 15 is divisible by 3.
A number is divisible by 4 if the number formed by the last two digits is divisible by 4.	316 is divisible by 4, since the last two digits (1 and 6) make a number that is divisible by 4 (16).
A number is divisible by 5 if the last digit is 0 or 5.	185 is divisible by 5, since the last digit is 5.
A number is divisible by 6 if it is divisible by both 2 and 3.	168 is divisible by 6, since it is divisible by both 2 and by 3.
A number is divisible by 7 if you can double the last digit, subtract it from the rest of the number, and the difference is divisible by 7.	203 is divisible by 7, because if you double 3 and subtract the number (6) from 20, the difference is 14. 14 is divisible by 7.
A number is divisible by 8 if the number formed by the last three digits is divisible by 8.	1,120 is divisible by 8, since 120 is divisible by 8.
A number is divisible by 9 if the sum of the digits is divisible by 9.	459 is divisible by 9, since the sum of the digits is 18 (4 + 5 + 9 = 18). 18 is divisible by 9.
A number is divisible by 10 if the last digit is 0.	2,380 is divisible by 10, since the last digit is 0.

Use the divisibility rules to determine if 5,168 is divisible by any numbers from 2–10.

NUMBER	DIVISIBLE BY	YES OR NO?	EXPLANATION
5,168	2	Yes	The last digit is 8.
5,168	3	No	Sum of the digits is 20, not divisible by 3.
5,168	4	Yes	68 is divisible by 4.
5,168	5	No	5,168 doesn't end with 5 or 0.
5,168	6	No	Not divisible by 3.
5,168	7	No	500 is not divisible by 7.
5,168	8	Yes	168 is divisible by 8.
5,168	9	No	Sum of the digits is 20, not divisible by 9.
5,168	10	No	5,168 doesn't end with 0.

5,168 is divisible by 2, 4, and 8.

Ask students to complete the chart below using the divisibility rules.

NUMBER	DIVISIBLE BY	YES OR NO?	EXPLANATION
9,042	2		
9,042	3		
9,042	4		
9,042	5		
9,042	6		
9,042	7		
9,042	8		
9,042	9		
9,042	10		

Divisibility rules can be used to find factors of large numbers and to determine if some numbers are prime or composite.

TEACHER NOTES: Prime and Composite Numbers

(Diagnostic Test Part I: Test Items 3, 4)

Review the definitions of prime and composite numbers with students. A **prime number** is a positive integer greater than 1 that has exactly one factor other than 1 (itself). Examples of prime numbers are 2, 3, 5, and 7.

Factors of Prime Numbers = {1, itself}

- Factors of 2 = {1, 2}   (only divisible by 2)
- Factors of 3 = {1, 3}   (only divisible by 3)
- Factors of 5 = {1, 5}   (only divisible by 5)
- Factors of 7 = {1, 7}   (only divisible by 7)

A **composite number** is a positive integer greater than 1 that has at least one factor other than 1 and itself. Examples of composite numbers are 4, 6, 10, and 25.

Factors of Composite Numbers = {1, factor 1, itself . . .}

- Factors of 4 = {1, 2, 4}   (only divisible by 2 and 4)
- Factors of 6 = {1, 2, 3, 6}   (only divisible by 2, 3, and 6)
- Factors of 10 = {1, 2, 5, 10}   (only divisible by 2, 5, and 10)
- Factors of 25 = {1, 5, 25}   (only divisible by 5 and 25)

TEACHING ACTIVITY: "Prime or Composite?" (Prime and Composite Numbers)

Students can find out whether a number is prime or composite either by using the divisibility rules or by finding all of the factors of the numbers. (**Note:** There are some exceptional numbers that do not follow any of the divisibility rules, but are still composite, such as **289**: 17 x 17 = 289.) Provide students with charts like the one below to practice finding prime and composite numbers.

NUMBER	FACTORS	DIVISIBLE BY	PRIME OR COMPOSITE?
18	{1, 2, 3, 6, 9, 18}	2, 3, 6, 9, 18	Composite
17	{1, 17}	17	Prime
22	{1, 2, 11, 22}	2, 11, 22	Composite
21	{1, 3, 7, 21}	3, 7, 21	Composite
59	{1, 59}	59	Prime

TEACHER NOTES: Exponents

(Diagnostic Test Part I: Test Items 5–7)

Ask students the following question: *"What is 2 to the 5th power?"*

Write students' responses on the board. Explain that a power is the product of multiplying a number by itself. A power is written with a base number and an exponent. The **base number** represents what number is to be multiplied and the **exponent** tells how many times the base number is to be multiplied by itself. The exponent is written as a small number above and to the right of the regularly sized base number.

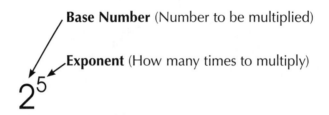

Base Number (Number to be multiplied)

Exponent (How many times to multiply)

2^5

NUMBER	READ AS	FACTOR AND STANDARD FORM	COMMON MISTAKE
2^5	Two to the fifth power	$2 \times 2 \times 2 \times 2 \times 2 = 32$	$2 \times 5 = 10$
3^2	Three squared	$3 \times 3 = 9$	$3 \times 2 = 6$
7^3	Seven cubed	$7 \times 7 \times 7 = 343$	$7 \times 3 = 21$
4^4	Four to the fourth power	$4 \times 4 \times 4 \times 4 = 256$	$4 \times 4 = 16$
5^2	Five squared	$5 \times 5 = 25$	$5 \times 2 = 10$
6^3	Six cubed	$6 \times 6 \times 6 = 216$	$6 \times 3 = 18$
8^2	Eight squared	$8 \times 8 = 64$	$8 \times 2 = 16$

The following rules apply to numbers with exponents of 0, 1, 2, and 3.

RULE	EXAMPLE
Any number (except 0) to the power of 0 is equal to 1.	$15^0 = 1$, $10^0 = 1$, $2^0 = 1$
The number 0 raised to any power is 0.	$0^2 = 0$, $0^5 = 0$, $0^3 = 0$
Any number to the power of 1 is equal to itself.	$6^1 = 6$, $9^1 = 9$, $20^1 = 20$
If a number is raised to the power of 2, it is read "squared."	3^2 is read as "three squared."
If a number is raised to the power of 3, it is read "cubed."	5^3 is read as "five cubed."

TEACHING ACTIVITY: "Exponent Chart"

Explain to students that numbers can be written in exponential form, factor form, and standard form.

Example: Exponential Form: 2^3
                  Factor Form: 2 x 2 x 2
                  Standard Form: 8

Instruct students to write the exponential form and the standard form of each number written in factor form in a chart like the one below. When students complete the chart, add a few numbers in standard form. Ask students to find what the numbers are in exponential form.

EXPONENTIAL FORM	FACTOR FORM	STANDARD FORM
	10 x 10 x 10	
	3 x 3 x 3 x 3 x 3 x 3	
	1 x 1 x 1 x 1 x 1 x 1 x 1	
	2 x 2 x 2 x 2 x 2	
	10 x 10 x 10 x 10 x 10 x 10	
	5 x 5 x 5	
	6 x 6	

TEACHER NOTES: Prime Factorization
(Diagnostic Test Part I: Test Items 8–10)

Review with students that factors are the numbers multiplied together to create a product. For example, the factors of 15 are 1, 3, 5, and 15, because 3 x 5 = 15 and 1 x 15 = 15. Remind students that 1 is a factor of all numbers. Students should understand that some numbers have more than one way of being factored. For example, 18 can be factored as 1 x 18, 2 x 9, and 3 x 6.

Explain to students that some numbers have only two factors: that number and 1. These are known as prime numbers. For example, 13 is a prime number because it can only be factored as 1 x 13. Composite numbers can be factored down to prime numbers. This is called prime factorization. For example, the prime factors of 8 are 2 x 2 x 2.

Students can find the prime factors of a given number either by making prime number factor trees or by using repeated division.

TEACHING ACTIVITIES "Prime Factor Trees" (Prime Factorization)

Demonstrate the following method of creating factor trees for students. Begin by asking students to find the prime factors of 24.

Step 1: Start with any two factors of 24. If the number is even, students will find it easiest to begin with the factor 2. Circle the prime factors.

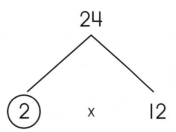

Step 2: 12 is not prime, so write two factors of 12. Circle the prime factors.

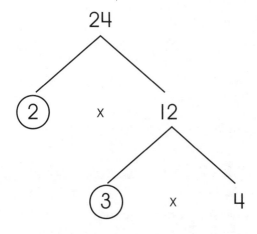

Step 3: 4 is not prime, so write two factors of 4. Circle the prime factors

Step 4: Write the prime factors of 24. Students should list factors in order from least to greatest.

2 x 2 x 2 x 3

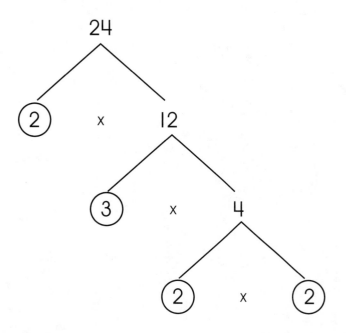

"Repeated Division" (Prime Factorization)

Students can also use repeated division to find prime factors. Demonstrate how to divide by prime numbers until the answer reaches 1. As with factor trees, students will find it easiest to begin with even numbers and divide by 2.

$$24 \div 2 = \textcircled{12} \qquad 12 \div 2 = \textcircled{6} \qquad 6 \div 2 = \textcircled{3} \qquad 3 \div 3 = \textcircled{1}$$

The prime factors of 24 are: 2 x 2 x 2 x 3.

Continue finding prime factors with students until they can complete the process on their own. Review basic division facts if necessary.

SPECIAL TEACHER NOTE

Many standardized tests ask students to show that they understand prime factorization without actually completing a factorization.

Example: Which answer shows the prime factorization of 36?

A.　2 x 2 x 3 x 3　　　　B.　2 x 3 x 3 x 3　　　　C.　2 x 18　　　　D.　4 x 3 x 3

Answer **A** is correct because all of the factors are prime and equal 36 when multiplied. Review questions like these with students to prepare for testing.

Divisibility Rules

Test Items 1–2

Determining Divisibility

Directions: Use the divisibility rules to determine which numbers in each problem are divisible by the given number.

1. Circle all of the numbers that are divisible by 6.

    30   53   75   5   54

    32   42   44   87   93

2. Circle all of the numbers that are divisible by 2.

    81   66   36   13   91

    624   8   65   870   157

3. Circle all of the numbers that are divisible by 8.

    680   1,452   2,360   3,400   2,234

    132   3,245   4,568   1,828   3,692

4. Circle all of the numbers that are divisible by 3.

    14   33   21   9   113

    56   833   34   18   7

5. Circle all of the numbers that are divisible by 5.

    467   82   15   45   560

    50   659   95   88   3,405

6. Circle all of the numbers that are divisible by 4.

    120   179   325   530   824

    643   768   340   116   262

7. Circle all of the numbers that are divisible by 7.

    456   323   514   455   257

    644   222   161   803   112

8. Circle all of the numbers that are divisible by 9.

    72   145   324   513   82

    26   90   621   314   251

CD-104227   •   Jump Into Math   •   © Carson-Dellosa

Find the Divisibility

Divisibility Rules

Test Items 1–2

Directions: Use the divisibility rules to test each number below. Write "Yes" on the line next to each number that will divide evenly into the given number.

1. 7,168

   Divisible by 2? _____

   Divisible by 3? _____

   Divisible by 4? _____

   Divisible by 8? _____

2. 9,042

   Divisible by 3? _____

   Divisible by 4? _____

   Divisible by 6? _____

   Divisible by 9? _____

3. 35,120

   Divisible by 2? _____

   Divisible by 4? _____

   Divisible by 5? _____

   Divisible by 8? _____

4. 477

   Divisible by 3? _____

   Divisible by 6? _____

   Divisible by 7? _____

   Divisible by 9? _____

5. 348

   Divisible by 2? _____

   Divisible by 4? _____

   Divisible by 6? _____

   Divisible by 9? _____

6. 23,624

   Divisible by 2? _____

   Divisible by 3? _____

   Divisible by 4? _____

   Divisible by 8? _____

7. 39,126

   Divisible by 2? _____

   Divisible by 3? _____

   Divisible by 4? _____

   Divisible by 8? _____

8. 120,458

   Divisible by 2? _____

   Divisible by 3? _____

   Divisible by 5? _____

   Divisible by 8? _____

9. 294

   Divisible by 2? _____

   Divisible by 3? _____

   Divisible by 6? _____

   Divisible by 7? _____

Divisibility Rules

Test Items 1–2

Divisibility Detective

Directions: Use the divisibility rules to test each number below. Write "Yes" on the line next to each number that will divide evenly into the given number.

1. 1,512

   Divisible by 2? _____
   Divisible by 5? _____
   Divisible by 7? _____
   Divisible by 8? _____
   Divisible by 9? _____

2. 54

   Divisible by 2? _____
   Divisible by 3? _____
   Divisible by 7? _____
   Divisible by 8? _____
   Divisible by 9? _____

3. 52,542

   Divisible by 3? _____
   Divisible by 4? _____
   Divisible by 6? _____
   Divisible by 7? _____
   Divisible by 8? _____

4. 906

   Divisible by 2? _____
   Divisible by 3? _____
   Divisible by 5? _____
   Divisible by 8? _____
   Divisible by 10? _____

5. 87

   Divisible by 2? _____
   Divisible by 3? _____
   Divisible by 7? _____
   Divisible by 8? _____
   Divisible by 9? _____

6. 73,688

   Divisible by 2? _____
   Divisible by 4? _____
   Divisible by 5? _____
   Divisible by 7? _____
   Divisible by 8? _____

7. 366

   Divisible by 2? _____
   Divisible by 3? _____
   Divisible by 6? _____
   Divisible by 8? _____
   Divisible by 9? _____

8. 7,221

   Divisible by 2? _____
   Divisible by 3? _____
   Divisible by 7? _____
   Divisible by 8? _____
   Divisible by 9 _____

9. 1,248

   Divisible by 2? _____
   Divisible by 3? _____
   Divisible by 5? _____
   Divisible by 6? _____
   Divisible by 8? _____

CD-104227 • Jump Into Math • © Carson-Dellosa

Prime or Composite?

Prime and
Composite Numbers

Test Items 3–4

Directions: Decide if each number is prime or composite. Then, circle the correct answer.

> A **prime number** has exactly two factors: 1 and itself.
> Example: 13 is prime because the only factors of 13 are 1 and 13.
>
> A **composite number** has more than two factors.
> Example: 8 is composite because the factors of 8 are 1, 2, 4, and 8.

1. **17**
   Prime   Composite

2. **14**
   Prime   Composite

3. **23**
   Prime   Composite

4. **32**
   Prime   Composite

5. **31**
   Prime   Composite

6. **53**
   Prime   Composite

7. **25**
   Prime   Composite

8. **18**
   Prime   Composite

9. **29**
   Prime   Composite

10. **52**
   Prime   Composite

11. **36**
   Prime   Composite

12. **2**
   Prime   Composite

13. **70**
   Prime   Composite

14. **45**
   Prime   Composite

15. **9**
   Prime   Composite

16. **97**
   Prime   Composite

17. **81**
   Prime   Composite

18. **69**
   Prime   Composite

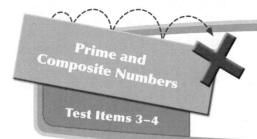

Prime and Composite Numbers

Test Items 3–4

Prime or Composite?

Directions: First, write all of the factors for each number. Then, write the numbers that the first number is divisible by. With this information, decide whether each number is prime or composite.

> **Remember:** A prime number has only two factors: I and itself. Composite numbers have more than two factors.

NUMBER	FACTORS	DIVISIBLE BY	PRIME OR COMPOSITE?
I. 27			
2. 15			
3. 17			
4. 19			
5. 42			
6. 31			
7. 22			
8. 41			
9. 37			
10. 55			

CD-104227 • Jump Into Math • © Carson-Dellosa

NAME: _____ DATE: _____

Exponential Form

Directions: Look at the example below. Then, complete the problems.

Example: An exponent is an easy way to write a number that is the product of many equal factors.

Exponential Form		Factor Form		Standard Form
2^5	=	2 x 2 x 2 x 2 x 2	=	32
10^3	=	10 x 10 x 10	=	1,000

Directions: Write the following numbers in exponential form.

1. 2 x 2 x 2 x 2 = _____

2. 3 x 3 x 3 = _____

3. 5 x 5 x 5 x 5 = _____

4. 4 x 4 x 4 x 4 x 4 x 4 = _____

5. 10 x 10 x 10 x 10 = _____

6. 2 x 2 x 2 x 2 x 2 x 2 x 2 = _____

7. 4 x 4 = _____

8. 3 x 3 x 3 x 3 x 3 = _____

9. 10 x 10 x 10 x 10 x 10 = _____

10. 5 x 5 x 5 x 5 x 5 = _____

Directions: Write the following numbers in factor form.

11. 3^3 = _____

12. 5^2 = _____

13. 2^5 = _____

14. 4^6 = _____

15. 10^0 = _____

16. 2^6 = _____

17. 3^4 = _____

18. 5^5 = _____

19. 10^3 = _____

20. 4^1 = _____

Directions: Write the following numbers in standard form.

21. 10 x 10 x 10 = _____

22. 5^2 = _____

23. 2^4 = _____

24. 2 x 2 x 2 x 2 x 2 = _____

25. 3^5 = _____

26. 5 x 5 x 5 x 5 = _____

The Truth About Exponents

Directions: Write "True" or "False" on the line next to each statement.

_____ 1. In 2^5, 2 is the exponent and the 5 is the base.

_____ 2. 2 x 2 x 2 x 2 is the same as 8.

_____ 3. 5^2 can be read, "five squared."

_____ 4. In 4^3, 3 is the exponent.

_____ 5. 125 is the same as 5^3.

_____ 6. 2^3 can be read, "two cubed."

_____ 7. 32 is the same as 2 x 2 x 2 x 2 x 2.

_____ 8. In 5^4, 5 is the base and 4 is the exponent.

_____ 9. 7^3 does not mean 7 x 3 = 21.

_____ 10. 3^5 can be read, "three to the fifth power."

_____ 11. 5 x 5 x 5 x 5 is the same as 4^5.

_____ 12. The base number is the number to be multiplied.

_____ 13. The exponent tells how many times to multiply the base.

_____ 14. 1,000,000 is the same as 10^6.

_____ 15. 4^5 can be read, "four times five."

CD-104227 • Jump Into Math • © Carson-Dellosa

NAME: _____   DATE: _____

Finding Prime Factors

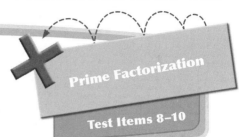

Directions: Use factor trees or repeated division to find the prime factors for each number below.

Prime factorization means to find all of the prime factors for a given number. You can find the prime factors of a given number by making a factor tree or by using repeated division.

Factor Tree

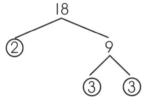

The prime factors are 2 x 3 x 3.

Repeated Division

18 ÷ **2** = ⑨   9 ÷ **3** = ③   3 ÷ **3** = ①

The prime factors are 2 x 3 x 3.

1.   120

           10   12

The prime factors are_____ .

2.   24

The prime factors are _____ .

3.   36

The prime factors are _____ .

4.   60

The prime factors are_____ .

5.   45

The prime factors are _____ .

6.   72

The prime factors are_____ .

NAME: _____ DATE: _____

Factor Trees

Directions: Use factor trees to find all of the prime factors for each number below. Then, list the prime factors.

1. 15

2. 33

3. 25

Prime Factors: _____

Prime Factors: _____

Prime Factors: _____

_____

_____

_____

4. 27

5. 24

6. 140

Prime Factors: _____

Prime Factors: _____

Prime Factors: _____

_____

_____

_____

7. 81

8. 96

9. 20

Prime Factors: _____

Prime Factors: _____

Prime Factors: _____

_____

_____

_____

Diagnostic Test: Integers

Directions: Write the answer to each question in the space provided.

Part I: Integer Concepts

1. What is the opposite of 27?

    _____

2. Write an integer to represent 200 less than 0.

    _____

3. What is the opposite of –10?

    _____

4. Write an integer to represent a loss of 3 yards in a football play.

    _____

5. Write an integer to represent a withdrawal of $125 from a bank account.

    _____

6. Use > or < to compare.

    $$-8 \bigcirc -2$$

7. Use > or < to compare.

    $$-4 \bigcirc -3$$

8. Use > or < to compare.

    $$-9 \bigcirc 0$$

9. Write the following integers in order from least to greatest.

    –5, 6, 0, –2, –1

    _____

10. Write the following integers in order from least to greatest.

    –1, –8, –6, 0, –4

    _____

TEACHER ASSESSMENT AREA

Directions: Shade the boxes that correspond to correct test items.

Skill	Item Number				
Writing Integers	1	2	3	4	5
Comparing and Ordering Integers	6	7	8	9	10

TOTAL CORRECT: _____

Teacher Notes and Activities

Background Information

In preparation for introduction to algebra, students should begin the study of positive and negative integers. Provide opportunities for students to represent situations involving positive and negative integers; to represent integers on a number line; to find opposite integers; and to order and compare integers.

TEACHER NOTES: Writing Integers
(Diagnostic Test Part I: Test Items 1–5)

Explore the following definitions with students.

- **Integer:** a whole number

- **Positive Integers:** all whole numbers greater than zero

- **Negative Integers:** all whole numbers less than zero

- **Opposite Integers:** two different integers that are the same distance from 0 on a number line

- **Zero:** zero is the only number that is not positive or negative

TEACHING ACTIVITY: "Understanding Positive and Negative"
(Writing Integers)

Ask students to stand next to their desks. Each desk represents zero. Instruct students to take 4 steps forward. This represents +4. Now ask students to take 4 steps backward. This represents –4. Students should now be next to their desks at zero. Explain that +4 and –4 are opposites. Show students a number line to further emphasize this relationship.

TEACHING ACTIVITY: "Understanding Positive and Negative"
(Identifying Positive and Negative Integers)

Give each student one index card with a plus sign and one index card with a minus sign. Then, read the statements listed below. Ask students to decide if each statement represents a positive (+) or negative (–) integer. They should each hold up a + or – card to describe the statement.

1. A loss of $1,000 on an investment
2. A deposit of $50 into a bank account
3. 15° below zero
4. A pay cut of $200
5. A gain of 5 pounds
6. 12 units to the left of zero on a number line
7. 1,500 feet below sea level
8. The opposite of –25
9. A loss of 10 pounds
10. The stock market goes up 225 points

TEACHER NOTES: Comparing and Ordering Integers

(Diagnostic Test Part 1: Test Items 6–10)

Use number lines to introduce positioning of positive and negative integers. Reinforce that zero is the point between positive and negative integers. All positive integers are to the right of zero, and all negative integers are to the left of zero. Remind students that zero is not positive or negative.

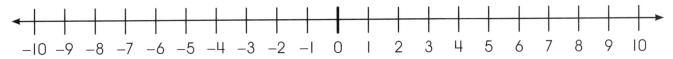

TEACHING ACTIVITIES:

"Ordering Integers" (Comparing and Ordering Integers)

Ask students to find and circle the following list of integers on a number line.

2, –5, –1, 5, –7, 0

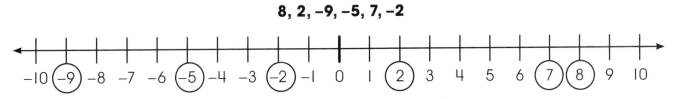

On a number line, the integers are in increasing order from left to right. When the integers are circled, students can clearly see them in the correct order.

Now, give students the following integers to find on a number line. Ask students to circle the integers, then order them from least to greatest.

8, 2, –9, –5, 7, –2

The numbers in order from least to greatest are –9, –5, –2, 2, 7, and 8.

"Comparing Integers" (Comparing and Ordering Integers)

Students can also use number lines to compare integers. For any two different places on a number line, the integer on the right is greater than the integer on the left.

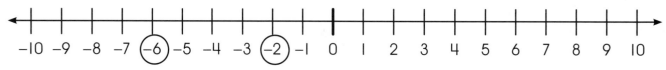

Compare –6 and –2.

Step 1: Find and circle –6 and –2 on a number line.

Step 2: The integer on the right is always larger, so **–6 < –2**.

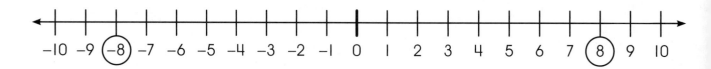

Compare 8 and –8.

Step 1: Find and circle 8 and –8 on a number line.

Step 2: The integer on the right is always larger, so **8 > –8**.

Ask students to use the number line method to compare the following integers, using > or <.

1. –3 ◯ –7   2. –3 ◯ –7   3. 6 ◯ –2   4. –9 ◯ 2

5. –2 ◯ –9   6. –5 ◯ –8   7. 10 ◯ –7   8. –1 ◯ –8

9. –9 ◯ –2   10. –8 ◯ 0   11. –1 ◯ 10   12. –1 ◯ –10

Describing with Integers

Writing Integers

Test Items 1–5

Directions: Write a positive or negative integer to describe each situation.

1. 5 units to the left of 10 on a number line _____

2. The stock market goes down 15 points _____

3. 12° below zero _____

4. The opposite of 27 _____

5. A football player loses 8 yards in a play _____

6. Withdraw $30 from a bank account _____

7. The price of gasoline goes up 25¢ _____

8. 45° above zero _____

9. 8 units to the left of 0 on a number line _____

10. A loss of 7 pounds _____

11. 6 units to the right of 0 on a number line _____

12. 800 feet above sea level _____

13. A pay cut of $1,000 _____

14. The stock market goes up 124 points _____

15. A gain of 8 pounds _____

16. 7 units to the left of 0 on a number line _____

17. Deposit $50 into a bank account _____

18. A profit of $45 from a bake sale _____

19. 185 feet below sea level _____

20. 15° below zero _____

Writing Integers

Test Items 1–5

Matching Integers

Directions: Write the letter of each integer on the line before its matching statement.

_____	1.	3,600 feet above sea level	A.	−5
_____	2.	A loss of $1,500 on an investment	B.	7
_____	3.	A deposit of $75 into a bank account	C.	−110
_____	4.	4 units to the left of −5 on a number line	D.	−8
_____	5.	A pay cut of $10 an hour	E.	75
_____	6.	A gain of 7 pounds	F.	120
_____	7.	9 units to the left of 4 on a number line	G.	10
_____	8.	A raise of $10 an hour	H.	−1,000
_____	9.	5 units to the right of 0 on a number line	I.	3,600
_____	10.	110 feet below sea level	J.	−4
_____	11.	7 units to the right of −10 on a number line	K.	−9
_____	12.	7 units to the right of −1 on a number line	L.	−54
_____	13.	8° below zero	M.	−1,500
_____	14.	The opposite of −120	N.	500
_____	15.	A loss of $1,000 on an investment	O.	−10
_____	16.	A quarterback is tackled for a loss of 4 yards	P.	6
_____	17.	A raise of $4,000 a year	Q.	5
_____	18.	54° below zero	R.	−13
_____	19.	A loss of 13 pounds	S.	−3
_____	20.	A deposit of $500 into a bank account	T.	4,000

Up and Down the Number Line

Writing Integers

Test Items 1–5

Directions: Use the number line to find and write the correct integer for each problem.

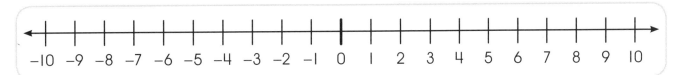

-10 -9 -8 -7 -6 -5 -4 -3 -2 -1 0 1 2 3 4 5 6 7 8 9 10

1. 5 units to the right of –4 _____

2. 4 units to the left of 10 _____

3. 8 units to the left of 5 _____

4. 7 units to the right of –7 _____

5. 9 units to the left of 2 _____

6. 10 units to the right of –4 _____

7. 12 units to the left of 9 _____

8. 10 units to the right of –10 _____

9. 5 units to the right of 0 _____

10. 10 units to the left of 1 _____

11. 8 units to the right of –1 _____

12. 6 units to the left of –4 _____

13. 6 units to the right of –4 _____

14. 3 units to the left of –3 _____

15. 3 units to the right of –3 _____

16. 5 units to the right of –9 _____

17. 9 units to the right of –5 _____

18. 4 units to the right of 5 _____

19. 4 units to the left of 3 _____

20. 8 units to the left of 1 _____

Comparing and
Ordering Integers

Test Items 6–10

Ordering Integers from Least to Greatest

Directions: Find the integers on the number line. Then, write them in order from least to greatest.

Example: –6, 7, 0, –2, 2

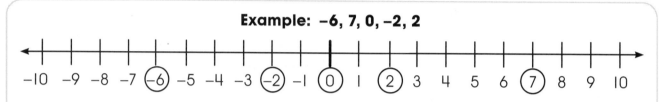

Write the integers from left to right: **–6, –2, 0, 2, 7**.

1. 0, 2, –5, 1, –9

   _____

2. –1, 1, –2, 2, 0

   _____

3. 4, –3, 2, –1, 0

   _____

4. 4, –10, 5, –2, –6

   _____

5. –6, –7, –3, 4, 6

   _____

6. –10, –8, 2, –4, 1

   _____

7. 8, –2, 2, 10, –8

   _____

8. 2, –4, 6, –8, 10

   _____

9. –10, –4, 8, –1, 2

   _____

10. –3, –4, 8, –1, 2

   _____

CD-104227 • Jump Into Math • © Carson-Dellosa

Order the Integers

Comparing and
Ordering Integers

Test Items 6–10

Directions: Order each set of integers from least to greatest.

1. 10, –14, –26, 4, –8, 22

    _____

2. 18, 6, –6, 16, –8, –10

    _____

3. –17, 34, 8, –31, 2, 5

    _____

4. 8, –2, 2, 12, –14, 9

    _____

5. –40, 44, –51, 24, 5, –48

    _____

6. 51, –17, 22, –36, –35, 25

    _____

7. 42, 21, –48, 72, –64, –20

    _____

8. –41, 54, –31, –79, 57, 80

    _____

9. –12, –8, 27, –11, 8

    _____

10. –41, –23, –31, 40, –21, 2

    _____

Comparing Integers

Directions: Compare each pair of integers. Write < or > in the circle.

You can use a number line to compare integers. For any two different places on a number line, the integer on the right is greater than the integer on the left.

Example: Compare –8 and 8.

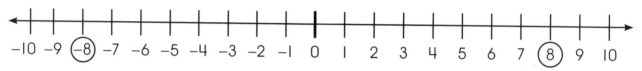

(Left: less than)   (Right: greater than)

–8 < 8

1. 15 ◯ –15   2. 12 ◯ –4   3. –9 ◯ 10   4. 16 ◯ 18

5. –13 ◯ –6   6. –7 ◯ –35   7. –13 ◯ –12   8. –39 ◯ –16

9. –5 ◯ –8   10. –3 ◯ 7   11. –22 ◯ –24   12. –46 ◯ –42

13. 10 ◯ 17   14. 15 ◯ –2   15. –14 ◯ –9   16. –3 ◯ –7

17. –21 ◯ –6   18. –33 ◯ –35   19. –47 ◯ –8   20. –9 ◯ 2

Diagnostic Test: Integers

Directions: Write the answer to each question in the space provided.

Part II: Adding and Subtracting Integers

1. $15 + 6 =$

2. $-14 + -45 =$

3. $5 + -15 =$

4. $-9 + 12 =$

5. $20 + -20 =$

6. $9 - 4 =$

7. $8 - (-20) =$

8. $7 - 10 =$

9. $-8 - 12 =$

10. $-6 - (-20) =$

TEACHER ASSESSMENT AREA

Directions: Shade the boxes that correspond to correct test items.

Skill	Item Number				
Adding Integers	1	2	3	4	5
Subtracting Integers	6	7	8	9	10

TOTAL CORRECT: _____

Teacher Notes and Activities

TEACHER NOTES: Adding Integers (Diagnostic Test Part II: Test Items 1–5)

The addition and subtraction operations with integers have some specific rules that are different from adding and subtracting whole numbers. Use manipulatives and visual representations to introduce and practice these new concepts. Helpful manipulatives for teaching integers include two-color counters and number lines.

Practice the following two-color counter activities before moving on to number line activities.

TEACHING ACTIVITIES: "Adding Positive Integers" (Adding Integers)

Use two-color counters to model the following positive-integer addition problems (the light side of the counters represents a positive value).

Rule: The sum of positive integers is always a positive integer.

Add: 2 + 3

$$2 \quad + \quad 3 \quad = \quad 5$$

Add: 4 + 3

$$4 \quad + \quad 3 \quad = \quad 7$$

"Use a Number Line to Add Positives" (Adding Integers)

Review with students that to add positive integers, they should find the first addend on a number line. Then, they must move to the right the number of spaces indicated by the second addend.

Rule: To add positive integers, always move to the right on the number line.

Add: 2 + 3

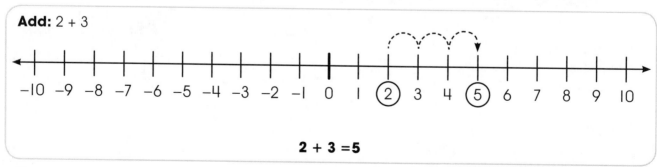

2 + 3 = 5

Add: 4 + 3

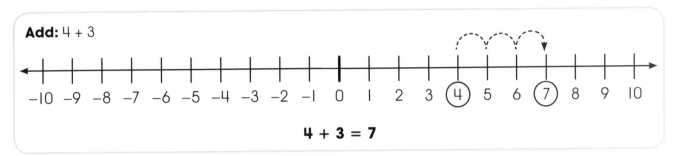

4 + 3 = 7

"Adding Negative Integers" (Adding Integers)

Use two-color counters to model the following negative-integer addition problems (the dark side of the counters represents a negative value).

Rule: The sum of negative integers is always a negative integer.

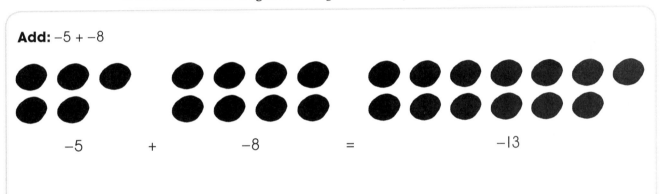

Add: −5 + −8

−5   +   −8   =   −13

Add: −2 + −6

−2   +   −6   =   −8

INTEGERS PART II: ADDING AND SUBTRACTING INTEGERS

"Use a Number Line to Add Negatives" (Adding Integers)

Explain to students that to add negative integers, they must find the first addend on a number line. Then, they should move to the left the number of spaces indicated by the second addend.

Rule: To add negative integers, always move to the left on the number line.

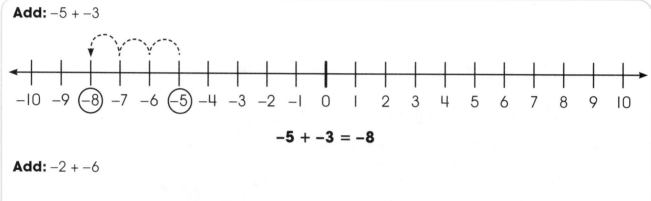

Add: $-5 + -3$

$$-5 + -3 = -8$$

Add: $-2 + -6$

$$-2 + -6 = -8$$

"Adding Positive and Negative Integers" (Adding Integers)

Rule: To add a positive integer and a negative integer, subtract the small number from the large number. The difference will take the sign of the larger number.

You can also use two-color counters to model the positive- and negative-integer addition problems. (Remember, positive integers are represented by the light side and negative integers by the dark side.)

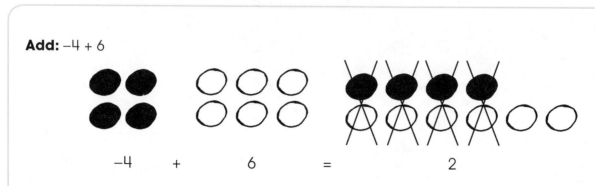

Add: $-4 + 6$

$$-4 \quad + \quad 6 \quad = \quad 2$$

$1 + -1 = 0$, so students can cross out "pairs."

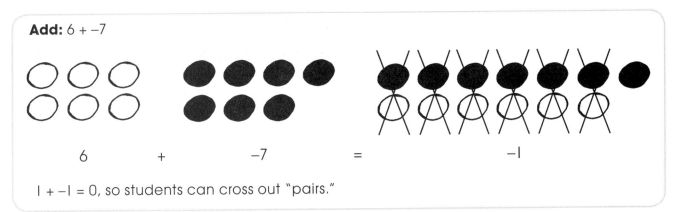

Add: 6 + −7

6   +   −7   =   −1

1 + −1 = 0, so students can cross out "pairs."

"Use a Number Line to Add Integers" (Adding Integers)

Explain to students that to add a positive integer and a negative integer, they must find the first addend on a number line. If the second addend is positive, they should move that number of spaces to the right. If the second addend is negative, they should move that number of spaces to the left.

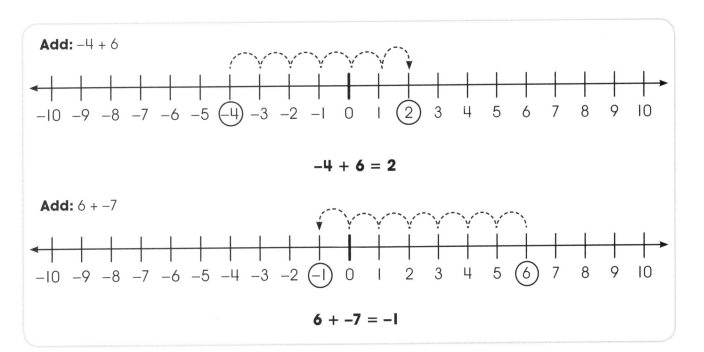

Add: −4 + 6

−4 + 6 = 2

Add: 6 + −7

6 + −7 = −1

TEACHER NOTES: Subtracting Integers (Diagnostic Test Part II: Test Items 6–10)

Use two-color counters and number lines to model subtraction of integers. The light side of the counters are positive and the dark side of the counters are negative. Reinforce the lessons by using number lines to show subtraction of integers, too.

TEACHING ACTIVITIES: "Adding Opposites" (Subtracting Integers)

Rule: To subtract an integer, add its *opposite*.

This rule can cause confusion for students. A thorough discussion and understanding of the meaning of the rule is necessary before students can practice subtraction of integers. One common error for students is to confuse the sign of the integer with the sign of the operation being performed. An effective remedy for this error is the use of parentheses around each integer. Explain this process with the example below.

---

5 – 2

Step 1: Write parentheses around each integer. Show all positive and negative signs.

$$(+5) - (+2)$$

Step 2: Find the opposite of the second addend. The opposite of +2 is –2.

Step 3: Rewrite the subtraction problem as an addition problem. Use the opposite of the second addend.

$$(+5) + (-2)$$

Step 4: Add.

(+5) + (–2) = (+3)

Students should continue to model with two-color counters and number lines until they fully understand this method.

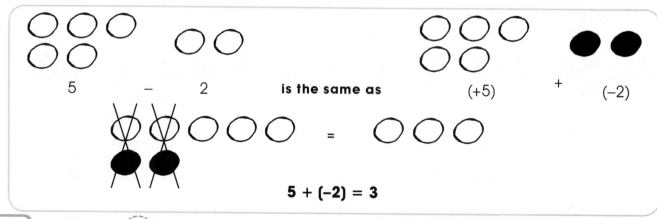

5 – 2

Step 1: Change 5 – 2 to an addition problem. Use the opposite of +2.

$$5 + (-2)$$

Step 2: Find 5 on the number line.

Step 3: Add –2. Start at 5 and move 2 spaces to the left.

5 + (–2) = 3

–5 – 2

Step 1: Write parentheses around each integer. Show all positive and negative signs.

$$(-5) - (+2)$$

Step 2: Find the opposite of the second addend. The opposite of +2 is –2.

Step 3: Rewrite the subtraction problem as an addition problem. Use the opposite of the second addend.

$$(-5) + (-2)$$

Step 4: Add.

(–5) + (–2) = (–7)

Model –5 – 2 with two-color counters:

Use the number line to solve. Start at –5 and move 2 spaces to the left.

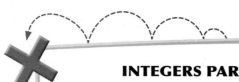
"Charting Integer Subtraction" (Subtracting Integers)

Show students a chart like the one below. Discuss the subtraction of integers rule. Note that the numbers in each problem are the same (3 and 7), but the integer signs alternate. Demonstrate how this changes the answer for each problem.

PROBLEM	ADD THE OPPOSITE	ANSWER
3 – 7	3 + (–7)	–4
3 – (–7)	3 + 7	10
–3 – 7	–3 + (–7)	–10
–3 – (–7)	–3 + 7	4

Practice with students the subtraction of integers rule using problems in the chart below. Allow students to use two-color counters or number lines until they feel comfortable using the rule. Record the results in a similar chart on a chalkboard.

PROBLEM	ADD THE OPPOSITE	ANSWER
9 – (–4)		
–7 – 10		
–9 – (–13)		
–2 – 1		
–3 – (–5)		
–3 – 5		
–5 – (–8)		
3 – 9		
7 – (–6)		
24 – (–24)		
1 – 7		
–1 – 7		
(–4) – (–4)		
4 – (–4)		
9 – 12		
–5 – 4		
–5 – (–4)		

NAME:_____   DATE:_____

Model Integer Addition

Directions: Use the two-color counters and the rules below to help you add integers.

The sum of positive integers is always a positive integer.	3 + 4 = 7
The sum of negative integers is always a negative integer.	−5 + (−2) = −7
To add a positive and a negative integer, subtract the smaller number from the larger number. The sum will take the sign of the larger number.	9 + (−2) = 7

◯ is positive.   ● is negative.

1. 3 + 4 = _____

2. −4 + −2 = _____

3. 7 + −3 = _____

4. 2 + 5 = _____

5. −3 + −2 = _____

6. 6 + −4 = _____

7. 7 + 3 = _____

8. −6 + −3 = _____

9. −4 + 6 = _____

10. 5 + −3 = _____

11. −10 + 4 = _____

12. −2 + 8 = _____

Integer Addition on a Number Line

Directions: Use the number line to help you add integers.

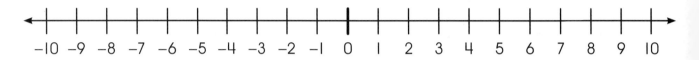

1. 4 + 6 = _____

2. −1 + −5 = _____

3. −4 + 8 = _____

4. −2 + −8 = _____

5. −6 + 8 = _____

6. 3 + 6 = _____

7. 5 + 4 = _____

8. −3 + −4 = _____

9. 4 + −8 = _____

10. −8 + 8 = _____

11. −6 + 5 = _____

12. 4 + −6 = _____

13. −2 + −6 = _____

14. 1 + 7 = _____

15. −8 + 9 = _____

 CD-104227 • Jump Into Math • © Carson-Dellosa

Adding Positive and Negative Integers

Adding Integers

Test Items 1–5

Directions: Use two-color counters to add the integers below.

1. $7 + 3 =$ _____

2. $-8 + -2 =$ _____

3. $10 + -8 =$ _____

4. $-10 + -5 =$ _____

5. $-1 + -9 =$ _____

6. $5 + -5 =$ _____

7. $-5 + -5 =$ _____

8. $5 + 5 =$ _____

9. $-3 + -6 =$ _____

10. $10 + 6 =$ _____

11. $15 + -11 =$ _____

12. $-4 + -8 =$ _____

13. $2 + 13 =$ _____

14. $15 + -13 =$ _____

15. $6 + -10 =$ _____

Directions: Use the number line to add the integers below.

16. $-8 + 7 =$ _____

17. $5 + -8 =$ _____

18. $8 + -7 =$ _____

19. $10 + -8 =$ _____

20. $5 + -7 =$ _____

21. $7 + -10 =$ _____

22. $-10 + 7 =$ _____

23. $-7 + -3 =$ _____

24. $-1 + -9 =$ _____

25. $5 + -10 =$ _____

26. $-8 + 9 =$ _____

27. $8 + -9 =$ _____

28. $5 + -13 =$ _____

29. $-4 + 12 =$ _____

30. $-10 + 12 =$ _____

NAME: _____   DATE: _____

Subtracting Integers

Test Items 6–10

Model
Integer Subtraction

Directions: Use two-color counters to subtract the integers. First, rewrite each problem as an addition problem. Then, draw the counters to represent each problem. Finally, write your answer in the chart.

> To subtract an integer, add its opposite.
>
> –7 – 5 is the same as –7 + (–5)   7 – 5 is the same as 7 + (–5)
>
> –7 – (–5) is the same as –7 + 5   7 – (–5) is the same as 7 + 5

WRITE YOUR ANSWER.	REWRITE AS ADDITION.	MODEL USING COUNTERS.
1. –8 – (–3) = **–5**	**–8 + 3**	●●●●●●●●●
2. 6 – (–4) =		
3. 4 – 5 =		
4. –5 – (–4) =		
5. –6 – 6 =		
6. 8 – 4 =		
7. 7 – (–4) =		
8. –9 – 5 =		
9. –3 – (–6) =		

172

CD-104227   •   Jump Into Math   •   © Carson-Dellosa

NAME: _____ DATE: _____

Integer Subtraction On a Number Line

Subtracting Integers

Test Items 6–10

Directions: First, change each subtraction problem to an addition problem. Then, write the answer on the next line.

–5 – 2

Change –5 – 2 to an addition problem. Use the opposite of 2.

–5 + (–2)

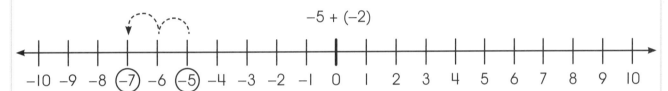

Find –5 on the number line.

Move 2 spaces to the left.

–5 – 2 = –7

1. –3 – (–2) = _____ = _____   2. –3 – 5 = _____ = _____

3. –7 – 2 = _____ = _____   4. 10 – 4 = _____ = _____

5. 3 – 7 = _____ = _____   6. –5 – (–12) = _____ = _____

7. –9 – (–9) = _____ = _____   8. 5 – 6 = _____ = _____

9. –8 – (–18) _____ = _____   10. –10 – (–11) = _____ = _____

Subtracting Integers

Test Items 6–10

More Integer Subtraction

Directions: Subtract the integers.

> **Remember:** To subtract an integer, add its opposite.

1. 8 – 7 =   _____

2. 12 – (–13) =   _____

3. –9 – (–6) =   _____

4. 14 – (–12) =   _____

5. 7 – 11 =   _____

6. –13 – (–20) =   _____

7. –21 – (–5) =   _____

8. –12 – (–8) =   _____

9. –9 – (–19) =   _____

10. 8 – 16 =   _____

11. –25 – (–24) =   _____

12. –19 – (–10) =   _____

13. 30 – 15 =   _____

14. –100 – (–10) =   _____

     CD-104227 • Jump Into Math • © Carson-Dellosa

Mixed Practice

Adding and
Subtracting Integers

Test Items 1–10

Directions: Use the addition and subtraction rules below to add and subtract integers.

The sum of positive integers is always a positive integer.	$3 + 4 = 7$
The sum of negative integers is always a negative integer.	$-5 + (-2) = -7$
To add a positive integer and a negative integer, subtract the smaller number from the larger number. The sum will take the sign of the larger number.	$9 + (-2) = 7$
To subtract an integer, add its opposite.	$9 - 7$ is the same as $9 + (-7) = 2$

1. $7 + 20 =$ _____

2. $-8 - (-10) =$ _____

3. $10 - (-11) =$ _____

4. $-30 + (-10) =$ _____

5. $42 + (-20) =$ _____

6. $-15 - (-8) =$ _____

7. $-22 - 12 =$ _____

8. $35 + 35 =$ _____

9. $16 + 12 =$ _____

10. $18 + (-16) =$ _____

11. $-40 - 15 =$ _____

12. $20 - 25 =$ _____

13. $-40 - (-50) =$ _____

14. $-24 + (-20) =$ _____

15. $32 + (-20) =$ _____

16. $55 - (-15) =$ _____

More Mixed Practice

Directions: Solve each of the following problems.

1. $7 + 14 =$ _____

2. $-9 - 11 =$ _____

3. $-15 - 15 =$ _____

4. $28 + -18 =$ _____

5. $17 - (-3) =$ _____

6. $-12 + -30 =$ _____

7. $-12 + 36 =$ _____

8. $-45 - 5 =$ _____

9. $23 + 48 =$ _____

10. $-23 + -48 =$ _____

11. $-125 - (-125) =$ _____

12. $34 + -24 =$ _____

13. $-44 + 22 =$ _____

14. $-26 - (-30) =$ _____

15. $33 - (-24) =$ _____

16. $70 - (-50) =$ _____

17. $-28 + 35 =$ _____

18. $17 - 19 =$ _____

19. $-45 + 20 =$ _____

20. $-44 - (-40) =$ _____

21. $33 - 35 =$ _____

22. $-150 - 160 =$ _____

CD-104227 • Jump Into Math • © Carson-Dellosa

Diagnostic Test: Exploring Percent

Directions: Write the answer to each question in the space provided.

Part I: Relating Fractions, Decimals, and Percent

1. Change the fraction to a percent.

   $\dfrac{34}{100}$ = _____ %

2. Change the fraction to a percent.

   $\dfrac{87}{100}$ = _____ %

3. Change the fraction to a percent.

   $\dfrac{3}{25}$ = _____ %

4. Change the fraction to a percent.

   $\dfrac{1}{5}$ = _____ %

5. Change the fraction to a percent.

   $\dfrac{7}{8}$ = _____ %

6. Change the decimal to a percent.

   0.47 = _____ %

7. Change the decimal to a percent.

   0.003 = _____ %

8. Change the decimal to a percent.

   0.018 = _____ %

9. Change the decimal to a percent.

   0.7 = _____ %

10. Change the decimal to a percent.

    1.25 = _____ %

TEACHER ASSESSMENT AREA

Directions: Shade the boxes that correspond to correct test items.

Skill	Item Number				
Changing Fractions to Percents	1	2	3	4	5
Changing Decimals to Percents	6	7	8	9	10

TOTAL CORRECT:_____

Teacher Notes and Activities

TEACHER NOTES: Changing Fractions to Percents
(Diagnostic Test Part I: Test Items 1–5)

When introducing percent, build on students' knowledge of fractions and decimals. Explain that percent means "out of 100," and is represented by the percent symbol (%). Use the following activity to show students that percent is an easy way to write fractions with a denominator of 100.

TEACHING ACTIVITY: "Introducing Percent" (Changing Fractions to Percent)

Write the following statement on a chalkboard: "80 out of 100 children prefer chocolate ice cream."

Explain to students that they can write this statement as a fraction, a decimal, and a percent. Write each version on the chalkboard to show students how they are related.

$$\frac{80}{100} \quad = \quad 0.80 \quad = \quad 80\%$$

$$\text{Fraction} \qquad \text{Decimal} \qquad \text{Percent}$$

Explain that to change a fraction with a denominator of 100 to a percent, students can simply write the numerator with a % symbol.

$$\frac{32}{100} = 32\% \qquad\qquad \frac{5}{100} = 5\%$$

Then, explain that if a fraction does not have a denominator of 100, there are two ways to change it to a decimal: the equivalent fraction method and the division method.

Equivalent Fraction Method

If a fraction does not have a denominator of 100, it is sometimes simplest to change the fraction to an equivalent fraction with a denominator of 100.

$$\frac{4}{5} = \frac{4 \times 20}{5 \times 20} = \frac{80}{100} = 80\% \qquad\qquad \frac{3}{25} = \frac{3 \times 4}{25 \times 4} = \frac{12}{100} = 12\%$$

$$\frac{3}{4} = \frac{3 \times 25}{4 \times 25} = \frac{75}{100} = 75\%$$

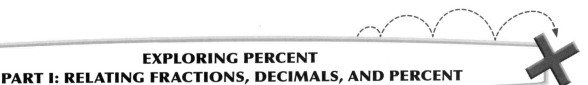

Division Method

Another way to change a fraction to a percent is to change it to a decimal first. Divide the numerator by the denominator. Then, move the decimal point two places to the right and write the percent symbol.

$$\frac{4}{5} = 5\overline{)4.00}^{\,0.80} = 80\% \qquad\qquad \frac{3}{25} = 25\overline{)3.00}^{\,0.12} = 12\%$$

$$\frac{3}{4} = 4\overline{)3.00}^{\,0.75} = 75\% \qquad\qquad \frac{7}{8} = 8\overline{)7.00}^{\,0.875} = 87.5\%$$

TEACHER NOTES: Changing Decimals to Percents
(Diagnostic Test Part I: Test Items 6–10)

Show students that decimals are easily changed to percents by moving the decimal point two places to the right (multiplying by 100) and writing the % symbol.

TEACHING ACTIVITIES
"Moving the Decimal" (Changing Decimals to Percents)

One percent and one hundredth are equivalent. This makes changing a decimal to a percent easy for students.

Explain that to change a decimal to a percent, students must simply multiply by 100 (move the decimal point two places to the right) and write the % symbol.

0.82 x 100 = 82%   0.03 x 100 = 3%   0.005 x 100 = 0.5%

0.82 = 82%   0.03 = 3%   0.005 = 0.5%

TEACHING ACTIVITIES
"Percent Practice" (Relating Fractions, Decimals, and Percent)

Ask students to practice changing fractions and decimals to percents with a chart like the one below.

FRACTION	DECIMAL	PERCENT
$\frac{47}{100}$	0.47	47%
$\frac{8}{100}$		
$\frac{1}{2}$		
$\frac{3}{4}$		
$\frac{3}{5}$		
$\frac{5}{8}$		

"Percents in Reverse" (Relating Fractions, Decimals, and Percent)

As students become more comfortable with changing fractions to percent and changing decimals to percent, instruct them to reverse the processes. Explain that they can do this by first removing the percent sign. Then, to make a fraction, they should write the number over a denominator of 100 and simplify. To make a decimal, they must simply move the decimal point two places to the left.

$$85\% \ = \ 0.85 \ = \ \frac{85}{100} \ = \ \frac{17}{20} \qquad\qquad 30\% \ = \ 0.30 \ = \ \frac{30}{100} \ = \ \frac{3}{10}$$

CD-104227 • Jump Into Math • © Carson-Dellosa

Fractions to Percents

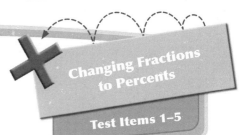

Changing Fractions to Percents

Test Items 1–5

Directions: Study the methods below. Then, follow the directions to solve each problem.

Equivalent Fraction Method

Change the fraction to an equivalent fraction with a denominator of 100.

$$\frac{4}{5} = \frac{4 \times 20}{5 \times 20} = \frac{80}{100} = 80\%$$

Division Method

Divide the numerator by the denominator. Then, move the decimal point two places to the right.

$$\frac{3}{4} = 4\overline{)3.00}^{\,0.75} = 75\%$$

Directions: Use the equivalent fraction method to change each fraction to a percent.

1. $\frac{11}{20}$ = _____   2. $\frac{1}{5}$ = _____   3. $\frac{9}{10}$ = _____   4. $\frac{2}{5}$ = _____

5. $\frac{23}{25}$ = _____   6. $\frac{17}{50}$ = _____   7. $\frac{3}{4}$ = _____   8. $\frac{4}{5}$ = _____

Directions: Use the division method to change each fraction to a percent.

9. $\frac{1}{4}$ = _____   10. $\frac{7}{10}$ = _____   11. $\frac{4}{5}$ = _____   12. $\frac{2}{5}$ = _____

13. $\frac{8}{25}$ = _____   14. $\frac{3}{15}$ = _____   15. $\frac{23}{50}$ = _____   16. $\frac{17}{20}$ = _____

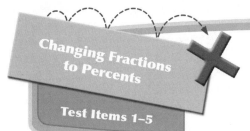

Fractions to Percents Practice

Directions: Use the equivalent fraction method or the division method to change each fraction to a percent. Round percents to the nearest hundredth, if needed.

1. $\dfrac{5}{16}$ = _____

2. $\dfrac{3}{8}$ = _____

3. $\dfrac{1}{10}$ = _____

4. $\dfrac{4}{5}$ = _____

5. $\dfrac{3}{4}$ = _____

6. $\dfrac{1}{4}$ = _____

7. $\dfrac{3}{25}$ = _____

8. $\dfrac{7}{8}$ = _____

9. $\dfrac{3}{10}$ = _____

10. $\dfrac{7}{16}$ = _____

11. $\dfrac{2}{3}$ = _____

12. $\dfrac{1}{12}$ = _____

13. $\dfrac{5}{6}$ = _____

14. $\dfrac{8}{16}$ = _____

15. $\dfrac{7}{12}$ = _____

16. $\dfrac{5}{8}$ = _____

17. $\dfrac{1}{3}$ = _____

18. $\dfrac{10}{12}$ = _____

CD-104227 • Jump Into Math • © Carson-Dellosa

Moving the Decimal

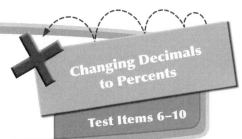

Changing Decimals
to Percents

Test Items 6–10

Directions: Study the example below. Then, change each decimal to a percent.

> To change a decimal to a percent, multiply by 100 (move the decimal point two places to the right) and write the % symbol.
>
> $$0.82 \times 100 = 82\%$$
>
> $$0.82 = 82\%$$

1. 0.35 = _____

2. 0.05 = _____

3. 0.77 = _____

4. 0.04 = _____

5. 1.34 = _____

6. 0.02 = _____

7. 0.16 = _____

8. 0.58 = _____

9. 0.08 = _____

10. 1.83 = _____

11. 0.43 = _____

12. 0.78 = _____

13. 1.09 = _____

14. 0.28 = _____

15. 0.06 = _____

16. 0.68 = _____

17. 1.56 = _____

18. 0.19 = _____

19. 0.01 = _____

20. 0.74 = _____

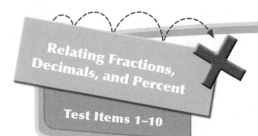

Changing Fractions to Decimals and Percents

Directions: Change each fraction to a decimal and a percent. Round to the nearest hundredth, if needed.

FRACTION	DECIMAL	PERCENT
1. $\dfrac{3}{5}$		
2. $\dfrac{5}{8}$		
3. $\dfrac{29}{100}$		
4. $\dfrac{8}{100}$		
5. $\dfrac{1}{2}$		
6. $\dfrac{3}{4}$		
7. $\dfrac{2}{3}$		
8. $\dfrac{7}{10}$		
9. $\dfrac{3}{10}$		
10. $\dfrac{51}{100}$		

CD-104227 • Jump Into Math • © Carson-Dellosa

Diagnostic Test: Exploring Percent

Directions: Write the answer to each question in the space provided.

Part I: Using Percent

1. 30% of 25 is what number?

_____

2. 80% of 40 is what number?

_____

3. 75% of 75 is what number?

_____

4. 24% of what number is 96?

_____

5. 20% of what number is 86?

_____

6. 40% of what number is 48?

_____

7. 28 is what percent of 41?

_____

8. 58 is what percent of 105?

_____

9. 107 is what percent of 148?

_____

10. What percent of 98 is 49?

_____

TEACHER ASSESSMENT AREA

Directions: Shade the boxes that correspond to correct test items.

Skill	Item Number			
Finding the Amount	1	2	3	
Finding the Base	4	5	6	
Finding the Percent	7	8	9	10

TOTAL CORRECT: _____

Teacher Notes and Activities

Background Information

Students must be familiar with the three most common percent problems. All three types of problems have the same basic parts: base, amount, and percent (rate). The base is the whole in a problem. The amount is the part of the whole being compared to the base. The rate is the ratio of the amount to the base. The rate is written as a percent. The following activities address the three most common types of percent problems.

TEACHER NOTES: Finding the Amount

(Diagnostic Test Part II: Test Items 1–3)

80% of 50 is: _____

What number is 80% of 50? _____

These questions represent the first type of percent problem, finding percent of numbers.

$$\text{Amount} = \text{Percent} \times \text{Base}$$

In the examples above, 80% is the percent and 50 is the base. In a percent problem in sentence form, the base always follows "of." Multiply the base by the percent to find the amount. The percent can be multiplied as a decimal or as a fraction.

80% of 50 is: _____

$$0.80 \times 50 = 40$$

or

$$\frac{80}{100} \times 50 = \frac{4000}{100} = 40$$

What number is 30% of 30? _____

$$0.30 \times 30 = 9$$

or

$$\frac{30}{100} \times 30 = \frac{900}{100} = 9$$

TEACHER NOTES: Finding the Base

(Diagnostic Test Part II: Test Items 4–6)

12 is 75% of what number? _____

75% of what number is 12? _____

These questions represent the second type of percent problem, finding the number that another number is a given percent of, or the base.

> Base = Amount ÷ Percent

In the examples above, 12 is the amount and 75% is the percent. Find the base in this type of problem by dividing the amount by the percent. Remind students that they may divide by a decimal or by a fraction.

12 is 75% of what number?

$$12 \div 0.75 = 16 \quad \textbf{or} \quad 12 \div \frac{75}{100} = 12 \times \frac{100}{75} = \frac{1200}{75} = 16$$

80% of what number is 20?

$$20 \div 0.80 = 25 \quad \textbf{or} \quad 20 \div \frac{80}{100} = 20 \times \frac{100}{80} = \frac{2000}{80} = 25$$

TEACHER NOTES: Finding the Percent

(Diagnostic Test Part II: Test Items 7–10)

What percent of 75 is 12? _____

12 is what percent of 75? _____

These questions represent the third type of percent problem, finding what rate a number is of another number, or the percent.

> Percent = Amount ÷ Base

In the examples below, 75 is the base and 12 is the amount. Find the percent in this type of problem by dividing the amount by the base.

What percent of 75 is 12?

$12 \div 75 = 0.16 = 16\%$

or

```
      0.16
75)12.00
  − 75
    450
  − 450
      0
```

27 is what percent of 90?

$27 \div 90 = 0.30 = 30\%$

or

```
      0.30
90)27.00
  − 270
      0
```

TEACHING ACTIVITY: "Identifying Percent Problems"

(Diagnostic Test Part II: Test Items 1–10)

Students should practice each type of percent problem separately until they can correctly identify and use the correct formula to solve the problem type. Do not mix the three problem types for practice until each student has mastered these tasks separately.

Display the three percent formulas on a bulletin board.

Amount = Percent x Base

Base = Amount ÷ Percent

Percent = Amount ÷ Base

To help students learn to identify each basic part, instruct them to practice by completing charts like the one below. Allow students to write a question mark (?) for unknown numbers.

PROBLEM	AMOUNT	BASE	PERCENT
1. What number is 50% of 12?	?	12	50%
2. 6 is 50% of 12.			
3. What number is 75% of 12?			
4. 12 is 75% of what number?			
5. 12 is what percent of 75?			
6. 75% of what number is 12?			
7. What percent of 75 is 12?			

EXPLORING PERCENT PART II: USING PERCENT

When students can identify basic percent problem parts, instruct them to complete charts like the one below. Students must identify which rule they should use to solve each problem. Ask students to write the appropriate rule next to each question.

Amount = Percent x Base

Base = Amount ÷ Percent

Percent = Amount ÷ Base

PROBLEM	RULE
1. How much is 50% of 12?	Amount = Percent x Base
2. 6 is 50% of what number?	
3. What number is 75% of 12?	
4. 12 is 75% of what number?	
5. 12 is what percent of 75?	
6. 75% of what number is 12?	
7. What percent of 75 is 12?	

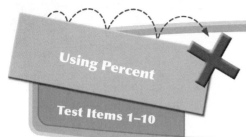

What Type of Percent Problem Is It?

Directions: Complete the chart below. For each problem, identify which number is the amount, which is the percent, and which is the base. Write each number in the correct column. If a number is not given, write a question mark (?). The first problem has been done for you.

PROBLEM	AMOUNT	BASE	PERCENT
1. 96 is 128% of what number?	96	?	128%
2. 27 is what percent of 90?			
3. How much is 30% of 12?			
4. 25% of how much is 125?			
5. 35 is 70% of what number?			
6. What percent of 150 is 52.5?			
7. 58 is what percent of 105?			
8. 36 is 12% of what number?			
9. 14% of how much is 78?			
10. 80% of 50 is how much?			
11. What percent of 240 is 170.4?			

Directions: Review the rules for solving percent problems. Then, write the number of the rule you should use to solve each of the following problems on the line provided.

> **Rule 1:** Amount = Percent x Base
> **Rule 2:** Base = Amount ÷ Percent
> **Rule 3:** Percent = Amount ÷ Base

_____ 1. What percent of 358 is 107?   _____ 2. 60% of 110 is what number?

_____ 3. 89 is 20% of how much?   _____ 4. What percent of 160 is 592?

_____ 5. 70% of 30 is how much?   _____ 6. 22% of how much is 440?

_____ 7. 72 is what percent of 120?   _____ 8. 38% of 96 is what number?

_____ 9. 125 is 25% of how much?   _____ 10. 75% of how much is 135?

NAME: _____ DATE: _____

Find the Amount

Directions: Use the formula below to solve each of the problems.

Amount = Percent x Base

80% of 50 is: _____   **or**   What number is 80% of 50?

0.80 x 50 = 40

1. 85% of 84 is: _____

2. What number is 99% of 82?

    _____

3. 339% of 29 is: _____

4. What number is 12% of 95?

    _____

5. 78% of 25 is: _____

6. What number is 50% of 88?

    _____

7. 60% of 80 is: _____

8. What number is 40% of 120?

    _____

9. 67% of 320 is: _____

10. What number is 35% of 1,200?

    _____

Finding the Amount

Test Items 1–3

"Of" Means Multiply

Directions: Use the formula below to solve the following percent problems.

> **Amount = Percent x Base**
>
> 35% of 70 = 0.35 x 70 = 24.5
>
> 125% of 200 = 1.25 x 200 = 250

1. 90% of 90 = _____

2. 60% of 130 = _____

3. 35% of 130 = _____

4. 25% of 180 = _____

5. 20% of 60 = _____

6. 170% of 150 = _____

7. 185% of 20 = _____

8. 70% of 30 = _____

9. 65% of 120 = _____

10. 75% of 300 = _____

11. 60% of 160 = _____

12. 110% of 400 = _____

13. 38% of 96 = _____

14. 48% of 108 = _____

15. 200% of 200 = _____

16. 75% of 500 = _____

CD-104227   •   Jump Into Math   •   © Carson-Dellosa

NAME: _____ DATE: _____

Clearance Sale

Directions: You are shopping. All of the items are on sale today. Find the amount of each discount. Then, subtract the amount of the discount from the original price to find the sale price.

Sale Today!

Computer Monitor $599.50. 20% off.

Step 1: Find the amount of the discount: 0.20 x $599.50 = $119.90

Step 2: Subtract the discount from the original price. $599.50 – $119.90 = $479.60

Sale Price: $479.60

---

1. Bicycle: $69.50. 37% off.

   Discount: _____

   Sale Price: _____

2. Computer Game: $63.20. 53% off.

   Discount: _____

   Sale Price: _____

3. DVD: $19.95. 25% off.

   Discount: _____

   Sale Price: _____

4. Skateboard: $29.95. 30% off.

   Discount: _____

   Sale Price: _____

5. Computer: $800.00. 33% off.

   Discount: _____

   Sale Price: _____

6. Running Shoes: $89.99. 12% off.

   Discount: _____

   Sale Price: _____

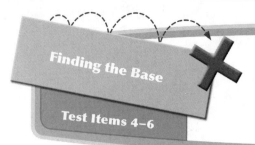

Finding the Base

Test Items 4–6

Find the Base

Directions: Use the formula below to solve the percent problems.

Base = Amount ÷ Percent

20 is 80% of what number?

20 ÷ 0.80 = 25

or

$$20 \div \frac{80}{100} = 20 \times \frac{100}{80} = \frac{2000}{80} = 25$$

1. 35 is 70% of what number?

   _____

2. 96 is 128% of what number?

   _____

3. 32 is 20% of what number?

   _____

4. 40 is 40% of what number?

   _____

5. 56 is 10% of what number?

   _____

6. 36 is 12% of what number?

   _____

7. 48 is 8% of what number?

   _____

8. 250 is 50% of what number?

   _____

9. 420 is 70% of what number?

   _____

10. 37 is 20% of what number?

   _____

CD-104227 • Jump Into Math • © Carson-Dellosa

NAME:_____ DATE:_____

Can You Find the Base Number?

Finding the Base

Test Items 4–6

Directions: Solve each problem to find the base. Round to the nearest hundredth.

Base = Amount ÷ Percent

360 is 12% of what number?   **or**   12% of how much is 360?

$360 ÷ 0.12 = 3,000$

1. 20% of how much is 89?

_____

2. 14% of how much is 78?

_____

3. 30% of how much is 68?

_____

4. 440 is 22% of what number?

_____

5. 80% of how much is 320?

_____

6. 450 is 48% of what number?

_____

7. 64% of how much is 280?

_____

8. 75% of how much is 135?

_____

9. 33% of how much is 91?

_____

10. 25% of how much is 125?

_____

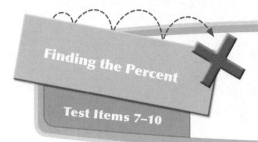

Finding the Percent

Test Items 7–10

Find the Percent

Directions: Solve each problem to find the percent. Round to the nearest hundredth.

Percent = Amount ÷ Base

12 is what percent of 75?　　　**or**　　　What percent of 75 is 12?

$$12 \div 75 = 0.16 = 16\%$$

$$75\overline{)12.00}^{\,0.16}$$

1. 27 is what percent of 90?

_____

2. What percent of 360 is 144?

_____

3. 38.4 is what percent of 48?

_____

4. 72 is what percent of 120?

_____

5. What percent of 150 is 52.5?

_____

6. 58 is what percent of 105?

_____

7. What percent of 348 is 107?

_____

8. 21.5 is what percent of 45?

_____

9. What percent of 240 is 170.4?

_____

10. What percent of 160 is 59.2?

_____

CD-104227 • Jump Into Math • © Carson-Dellosa

Find the Percent of the Discount

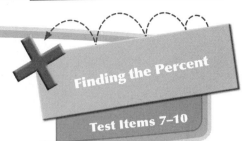

Finding the Percent

Test Items 7–10

Directions: Let's go shopping. Each item lists the original price and the discount amount. Find the percent of each discount. Then, order the discount percents from greatest to least.

Electric Car

Original Price: $280   Discount Amount: $140

Percent = Amount ÷ Base

$$140 \div 280 = 0.50 = 50\%$$

$$280\overline{)140.00}^{\,0.50}$$

Percent Discount: 50%

1. DVD
    Original Price: $24.50
    Discount Amount: $7.35
    Percent Discount: _____

2. Computer Game
    Original Price: $50.00
    Discount Amount: $14.50
    Percent Discount: _____

3. Running Shoes
    Original Price: $124.99
    Discount Amount: $41.25
    Percent Discount: _____

4. Mountain Bike
    Original Price: $159.60
    Discount Amount: $63.84
    Percent Discount: _____

5. Laptop Computer
    Original Price: $699.50
    Discount Amount: $349.75
    Percent Discount: _____

6. Amusement Park Ticket
    Original Price: $36.75
    Discount Amount: $7.35
    Percent Discount: _____

Which item has the best deal? List the items in order from greatest percent discount to least percent discount.

1. _____

2. _____

3. _____

4. _____

5. _____

6. _____

NAME: _____ DATE: _____

End of Book Test

Directions: Read the following problems. Circle the letter beside the correct answer to each question. Use a separate sheet of paper to work each problem.

1. Multiply.

   4,237
   x   5

   A. 21,185
   B. 21,085
   C. 20,185
   D. 20,085

2. Multiply.

   3.55
   x 0.7

   A. 2.485
   B. 24.85
   C. 0.2485
   D. 42.85

3. Subtract.

   $\frac{7}{8} - \frac{1}{6}$

   A. $\frac{15}{24}$

   B. $\frac{34}{48}$

   C. $1\frac{34}{48}$

   D. $\frac{17}{24}$

4. 5,168 is divisible by which numbers?

   A. 2, 3, 4, 8
   B. 2, 3, 8
   C. 2, 4, 8
   D. 4, 8, 10

5. Write the integers in order from least to greatest.

   −4, 0, −8, −1, −6

   A. 0, −1, −4, −6, −8
   B. −8, −6, −4, −1, 0
   C. 0, −8, −6, −4, −1
   D. −8, −6, −1, −4, 0

6. Write 0.024 as a percent.

   A. 2.4%
   B. 24%
   C. 02%
   D. 0.24

7. The underlined digits are what period?

   3,716,089,342

   A. Ones
   B. Thousands
   C. Millions
   D. Hundred Thousands

8. Divide.

   40)9,134

   A. 228
   B. 208 R 4
   C. 238 R 4
   D. 228 R 14

CD-104227 • Jump Into Math • © Carson-Dellosa

9. Add and simplify.

$$\frac{5}{8} + \frac{4}{9}$$

    A. $\frac{9}{72}$

    B. $1\frac{5}{72}$

    C. $1\frac{9}{72}$

    D. $1\frac{6}{72}$

10. Divide and simplify.

$$10 \div \frac{2}{3}$$

    A. $15\frac{1}{3}$

    B. 15

    C. $6\frac{2}{3}$

    D. $15\frac{2}{3}$

11. What is the opposite of 25?

    A. $\frac{25}{1}$

    B. $\frac{1}{25}$

    C. -25

    D. 0.25

12. What is the place value of the underlined digit?

$$635.7\underline{2}4$$

    A. Thousandths
    B. Hundredths
    C. Tens
    D. Tenths

13. Divide.

$$4\overline{)9.76}$$

    A. 24.4
    B. 2.44
    C. 244
    D. 2.43 R 3

14. Multiply and simplify.

$$4\frac{1}{4} \times 3\frac{2}{3}$$

    A. $15\frac{7}{12}$

    B. $12\frac{2}{12}$

    C. $15\frac{2}{12}$

    D. $12\frac{1}{6}$

15. Add.

$$-8 + 11$$

    A. -3
    B. 19
    C. 3
    D. -19

16. Multiply.

  57 x 34

    A. 399
    B. 1,938
    C. 1,848
    D. 1,399

17. Subtract and simplify.

  $6 \frac{3}{4} - 2 \frac{1}{2}$

    A. $4 \frac{3}{4}$

    B. $4 \frac{1}{4}$

    C. $4 \frac{2}{4}$

    D. $4 \frac{1}{2}$

18. Write 5 x 5 x 5 x 5 in exponential form.

    A. 4^5
    B. 625
    C. 5^4
    D. 5^2

19. Divide.

  $34\overline{)695}$

    A. 23 R 5
    B. 20 R 15
    C. 21 R 2
    D. 19 R 30

20. Divide and simplify.

  $5 \frac{2}{3} \div 3 \frac{1}{4}$

    A. $\frac{68}{39}$

    B. $2 \frac{5}{12}$

    C. $18 \frac{5}{12}$

    D. $1 \frac{29}{39}$

21. 65% of what number is 32.5?

    A. 2
    B. 50
    C. 21.13
    D. 40

22. Add and simplify.

  $3 \frac{1}{3} + 4 \frac{3}{5}$

    A. $7 \frac{14}{15}$

    B. $7 \frac{4}{8}$

    C. $7 \frac{1}{2}$

    D. $8 \frac{14}{15}$

23. What is the value of the underlined digit?

    475,796,737,508

    A. 7 billion
    B. 7 hundred thousand
    C. 7 hundred million
    D. 7 thousand

24. What are the prime factors of 24?

    A. 2 x 2 x 6
    B. 2 x 2 x 2 x 3
    C. 2 x 2 x 3
    D. 4 x 2 x 3

25. Write the decimals in order from greatest to least.

    0.45, 0.54, 0.05, 0.04

    A. 0.54, 0.45, 0.04, 0.05
    B. 0.54, 0.05, 0.04, 0.45
    C. 0.54, 0.45, 0.05, 0.04
    D. 0.54, 0.05, 0.45, 0.04

26. What is the standard form of 2^6?

    A. 64
    B. 12
    C. 32
    D. 36

27. Multiply.

    $$\begin{array}{r} 5.36 \\ \times\quad 6 \\ \hline \end{array}$$

    A. 321.6
    B. 3.216
    C. 32.16
    D. 32.36

28. Subtract.

    $-6 - 3$

    A. -9
    B. -3
    C. 3
    D. 9

29. Divide.

    $3.8\overline{)4.25}$

    A. 0.112
    B. 112
    C. 11.2
    D. 1.12

30. Multiply.

    $$\frac{3}{5} \times \frac{3}{4}$$

    A. $\frac{6}{9}$

    B. $\frac{6}{20}$

    C. $\frac{9}{20}$

    D. $\frac{12}{15}$

Answer Key

PAGES 7–8 (DIAGNOSTIC TEST)

1. 2; 2. billions; 3. thousands; 4. millions; 5. billion, million, thousand; 6. 2,045,678,901; 7. ten billions; 8. 900,000,000; 9. 3,216,780,145; 10. 3,000,000,000 + 70,000,000 + 1,000,000 + 500,000 + 40,000 + 2,000 + 800 + 90 + 6

PAGE 11

1. 5, 2. 9, 3. 6, 4. 0, 5. 4, 6. 3, 7. 5, 8. 3, 9. 8, 10. 3, 11. 9, 12. 6, 13. 5, 14. 7

PAGE 12

1. hundred thousands, 600,000; 2. millions, 4,000,000; 3. hundred millions, 300,000,000; 4. millions, 6,000,000; 5. millions, 7,000,000; 6. hundred millions, 800,000,000; 7. ten billions, 70,000,000,000; 8. billions, 4,000,000,000

PAGE 13

1. seven million one hundred fifty-one thousand seven hundred forty-one, 7 million 151 thousand 741, 7,000,000 + 100,000 + 50,000 + 1,000 + 700 + 40 + 1; 2. twenty-three million four hundred thirty-two thousand two hundred thirty-one, 23 million 432 thousand 231, 20,000,000 + 3,000,000 + 400,000 + 30,000 + 2,000 + 200 +·30 + 1; 3. fifty million two hundred sixty-three thousand one hundred nine, 50 million 263 thousand 109, 50,000,000 + 200,000 + 60,000 + 3,000 + 100 + 9; 4. seven billion seven hundred eighty million five hundred thousand five hundred forty-five, 7 billion 780 million 500 thousand 545, 7,000,000,000 + 700,000,000 + 80,000,000 + 500,000 + 500 + 40 + 5

PAGE 14

1. B, 2. B, 3. A, 4. D, 5. B, 6. C, 7. B

PAGES 15–16 (DIAGNOSTIC TEST)

1. hundredths; 2. 3.358; 3. 234.57; 4. tenths; 5. 315.35; 6. 10 + 7 + 3/10 + 2/100 + 8/1000; 7. >; 8. <; 9. 0.54, 0.45, 0.05, 0.04; 10. 6.54, 5.56, 4.65, 4.56, 4.44

PAGE 21

1. tenths, 2. hundredths, 3. thousandths, 4. tens, 5. thousandths, 6. tenths

PAGE 22

1. 3.358; 2. 6.781; 3. 315.12; 4. 9.768; 5. 10 + 7 + 3/10 + 2/100 + 8/1000; 6. 4.510; 7. 29.005

PAGE 23

1. 2.1, 2 + 1/10, two and one tenth; 2. 5.32, 5 + 3/10 + 2/100, five and thirty-two hundredths; 3. 0.28, 2/10 + 8/100, twenty-eight hundredths; 4. 8.045, 8 + 4/100 + 5/1,000, eight and forty-five thousandths; 5. 3.47, 3 + 4/10 + 7/100, three and forty-seven hundredths; 6. 1.15, 1 + 1/10 + 5/100, one and fifteen hundredths; 7. 2.503, 2 + 5/10 + 3/1,000, two and five hundred three thousandths; 8. 7.32, 7 + 3/10 + 2/100, seven and thirty-two hundredths; 9. 4.222, 4 + 2/10 + 2/100 + 2/1,000, four and two hundred twenty-two thousandths; 10. 8.6, 8 + 6/10, eight and six tenths

PAGE 24

1. H, 2. F, 3. B, 4. D, 5. G, 6. A, 7. E, 8. I, 9. C

PAGE 25

1. <, 2. <, 3. <, 4. >, 5. >, 6. <, 7. <, 8. >, 9. <, 10. >, 11. =, 12. =, 13. >, 14. <, 15. <

PAGE 26

1. >, 2. >, 3. >, 4. >, 5. <, 6. <, 7. =, 8. >, 9. >, 10. <, 11. <, 12. <, 13. <, 14. =, 15. >, 16. <, 17. <, 18. =, 19. >, 20. >, 21. =

PAGE 27

1. 0.80, 0.08, 0.008; 2. 3.6, 3.36, 3.016; 3. 5.7, 5.07, 5.007; 4. 9.4, 9.04, 0.94; 5. 65.03, 6.503, 6.053; 6. 7.6, 0.706, 0.7, 0.07; 7. 5.50, 5.05, 0.55, 0.055; 8. 16.461, 16.46, 16.457, 16.45; 9. 0.458, 0.4508, 0.4058, 0.0458; 10. 64.04, 6.4, 0.604, 0.064

PAGE 28

Shaded problems: 2., 3., 6., 7., 9., 10., 11.

PAGE 29 (DIAGNOSTIC TEST)

1. 300; 2. 3,200; 3. 21,000; 4. 3,445; 5. 14,622; 6. 522; 7. 2,924; 8. 1,323; 9. 21,286; 10. 16,388

PAGE 33

1. 80, 2. 120, 3. 160, 4. 200, 5. 100, 6. 150, 7. 200, 8. 250, 9. 180, 10. 240, 11. 300, 12. 360, 13. 280, 14. 350, 15. 420, 16. 490

PAGE 34

1. 600; 2. 1,200; 3. 2,000; 4. 2,000; 5. 1,000; 6. 1,500; 7. 2,400; 8. 2,500; 9. 1,800; 10. 2,800; 11. 3,500; 12. 3,600; 13. 3,200; 14. 4,000; 15. 4,800; 16. 5,600

PAGE 35

1. 6,000; 2. 12,000; 3. 20,000; 4. 16,000; 5. 15,000; 6. 20,000; 7. 25,000; 8. 30,000; 9. 24,000;

PAGE 35 (CONTINUED)

10. 30,000; 11. 42,000; 12. 49,000;
13. 40,000; 14. 48,000; 15. 56,000;
16. 64,000

PAGE 36

1. 180, 2. 175, 3. 176, 4. 216, 5. 140,
6. 195, 7. 235, 8. 275, 9. 216,
10. 270, 11. 348, 12. 378, 13. 322,
14. 385, 15. 441, 16. 525

PAGE 37

1. 1,024; 2. 3,115; 3. 3,296; 4. 5,913;
5. 2,185; 6. 2,976; 7. 3,445; 8. 5,271;
9. 1,938; 10. 3,324; 11. 4,584;
12. 5,292

PAGE 38

1. 7,305; 2. 16,225; 3. 7,370;
4. 25,956; 5. 15,616; 6. 26,785;
7. 33,224; 8. 31,494; 9. 49,056;
10. 52,712; 11. 51,681; 12. 49,232

PAGE 39

1. 420, 2. 319, 3. 264, 4. 385,
5. 660, 6. 492, 7. 324, 8. 583,
9. 588, 10. 539, 11. 682, 12. 864,
13. 336, 14. 814, 15. 600, 16. 996,
17. 396, 18. 825, 19. 648, 20. 605

PAGE 40

1. 1,056; 2. 1,014; 3. 952; 4. 1,530;
5. 1,595; 6. 2,013; 7. 1,995; 8. 2,835;
9. 1,728; 10. 1,960; 11. 1,848;
12. 1,947; 13. 2,772; 14. 2,989;

PAGE 40 (CONTINUED)

15. 2,494; 16. 1,856; 17. 2,405;
18. 3,082; 19. 3,105; 20. 3,808

PAGE 41

Shaded problems: 1., 3., 5., 8., 9.

PAGE 42

1. 4,945; 2. 1,716; 3. 11,264;
4. 7,584; 5. 22,825; 6. 11,856;
7. 23,352; 8. 13,936; 9. 26,685;
10. 26,640; 11. 27,404; 12. 38,350

PAGE 43

1. 9,600; 2. 15,134; 3. 43,036;
4. 18,252; 5. 26,460; 6. 49,595;
7. 26,588; 8. 38,759; 9. 49,136;
10. 50,456; 11. 37,968; 12. 44,352;
13. 45,864; 14. 62,320; 15. 47,475;
16. 31,768; 17. 72,105; 18. 54,852;
19. 57,442; 20. 60,371

PAGE 44

1. 10,989, D.; 2. 11,100, F.; 3. 35,156,
K.; 4. 60,384, N.; 5. 43,340, J.;
6. 57,472, G.; 7. 37,848, L.;
8. 68,328, A.; 9. 44,191, E.;
10. 29,138, B.; 11. 55,080, C.;
12. 41,797, M.; 13. 80,784, O.;
14. 64,548, H.; 15. 30,726, I.

PAGE 45 (DIAGNOSTIC TEST)

1. 7 R 3; 2. 29 R 2; 3. 158 R 3;
4. 777 R 2; 5. 7,881; 6. 228 R 14;
7. 33 R 12; 8. 304 R 11; 9. 460 R 8;
10. 1,395 R 1

PAGE 51

1. 7 R 2, 2. 4 R 4, 3. 29 R 2,
4. 16 R 1, 5. 23 R 2, 6. 10 R 1,
7. 15 R 3, 8. 4 R 5, 9. 17 R 1,
10. 16 R 1, 11. 9 R 1, 12. 12 R 2

PAGE 52

1. 6 R 3, 2. 9 R 4, 3. 8 R 2, 4. 15 R 4,
5. 7 R 4, 6. 21 R 1, 7. 17 R 1,
8. 9 R 3, 9. 12 R 1, 10. 17 R 3,
11. 11 R 2, 12. 28 R 1, 13. 22 R 1,
14. 28

PAGE 53

1. C, 2. D, 3. A, 4. B, 5. C, 6. A,
7. D, 8. A, 9. C

PAGE 54

1. 53 R 2, 2. 78 R 3, 3. 89 R 1,
4. 77 R 6, 5. 42 R 2, 6. 76 R 1,
7. 90, 8. 79 R 6, 9. 177 R 2,
10. 159 R 3, 11. 81, 12. 396

PAGE 55

1. 1,660 R 2; 2. 1,417; 3. 1,561 R 2;
4. 928; 5. 838 R 6; 6. 1,269 R 5

PAGE 56

1. 2,797 R 4; 2. 7,396 R 2;
3. 7,099 R 3; 4. 6,837 R 7;
5. 14,301 R 1; 6. 6,690 R 5

PAGE 57

1. 24 R 6, 2. 22 R 5, 3. 27 R 3,
4. 12 R 1, 5. 22 R 4, 6. 31 R 7,
7. 34 R 2, 8. 18 R 5, 9. 17 R 9

PAGE 58

1. 778, 2. 443 R 3, 3. 218 R 3,
4. 45 R 6, 5. 83 R 6, 6. 157 R 2,
7. 140, 8. 73 R 10, 9. 150 R 10,
10. 142 R 10, 11. 72 R 5, 12. 143 R 9

PAGE 59

1. B, 2. D, 3. A, 4. B, 5. B, 6. D,
7. C, 8. A, 9. C, 10. A

PAGE 60

1. 26 R 5, 2. 21 R 21, 3. 20 R 8,
4. 13 R 1, 5. 21 R 26, 6. 22 R 4,
7. 11 R 47, 8. 21 R 6, 9. 23,
10. 16 R 2, 11. 15 R 10, 12. 18 R 4

PAGE 61

1. 204 R 7, 2. 318 R 18, 3. 202 R 3,
4. 98 R 19, 5. 270 R 8, 6. 147 R 20,
7. 106 R 26, 8. 48 R 8, 9. 130 R 42,
10. 112 R 25, 11. 108 R 59,
12. 100 R 7

PAGE 62

1. 3,031; 2. 2,466; 3. 1,232 R 18;
4. 1,172 R 5; 5. 883 R 14; 6. 1,387;
7. 2,674 R 14; 8. 450 R 8;
9. 456 R 6; 10. 951 R 46;
11. 451 R 55; 12. 881 R 26

PAGE 63 (DIAGNOSTIC TEST)

1. 5.4; 2. 9.6; 3. 13,500; 4. 1,025;
5. 27.25; 6. 8.25; 7. 0.06; 8. 1.968;
9. 0.1220; 10. 0.54125

PAGE 68

1. 3.6; 2. 2.5; 3. 5.6; 4. 2.1; 5. 7.2;
6. 1.8; 7. 2.4; 8. 4.2; 9. 2.8; 10. 4.8;
11. 4.8; 12. 13.5; 13. 13.8; 14. 9;
15. 26.4; 16. 9.6

ANSWER KEY

PAGE 69

1. 0.63; 2. 0.072; 3. 0.81; 4. 0.045;
5. 2.64; 6. 1.59; 7. 2.35; 8. 3.90;
9. 0.042; 10. 0.328; 11. 6.37;
12. 6.84; 13. 4.76; 14. 77.4; 15. 52.5;
16. 79.2

PAGE 70

1. 2.5; 2. 13.5; 3. 34.5; 4. 43.7;
5. 61.3; 6. 85.8; 7. 25.0; 8. 435;
9. 538; 10. 6,660; 11. 7,930;
12. 8,230; 13. 250; 14. 3,490;
15. 9,610; 16. 86,400;
17. 77,600; 18. 92,500

PAGE 71

1. 14.84; 2. 0.98; 3. 37.84; 4. 0.0280;
5. 0.5625; 6. 0.4012; 7. 0.00559;
8. 3.374; 9. 204.36; 10. 43.26,
11. 1.722; 12. 3.9075

PAGE 72

1. 35.802; 2. 16.324; 3. 14.952;
4. 31.178; 5. 0.843; 6. 34.204;
7. 12.138; 8. 35.802; 9. 0.2408;
10. 1.9992; 11. 118.712; 12. 0.07897

PAGE 73

1. 5, 2.52399; 2. 4, 75.1185;
3. 5, 0.83424; 4. 4, 10.3333; 5. 4,
05.3038; 6. 4, 86.8296; 7. 4, 6.9248;
8. 4, 1.1635; 9. 3, 2238.288;
10. 4, 54.8964; 11. 4, 7.5204; 12. 4,
23.4564

PAGE 74 (DIAGNOSTIC TEST)

1. 3.30; 2. 0.82; 3. 1.934; 4. 12.013;
5. 13.6; 6. 0.70; 7. 1.118; 8. 3.40;
9. 5.046; 10. 21.455

PAGE 79

1. 0.73; 2. 1.16; 3. 1.27; 4. 1.75;
5. 1.67; 6. 1.93; 7. 0.58125; 8. 0.54

PAGE 80

1. 0.55; 2. 5.5; 3. 27.4; 4. 13.6;
5. 12.7; 6. 6.1; 7. 2.59; 8. 12.55;
9. 0.35; 10. 3.3; 11. 0.55; 12. 3.22

PAGE 81

1. $6.70; 2. $2.50; 3. $6.10;
4. $6.75; 5. $7.22; 6. 15 pounds

PAGE 82

1. 1.35; 2. 1.4; 3. 0.7; 4. 3.3; 5. 3.4;
6. 3,070; 7. 2.3; 8. 62; 9. 12

PAGE 83

1. 1.118; 2. 7.3; 3. 9.2; 4. 62; 5. 6.8;
6. 55.5; 7. 1,386; 8. 11; 9. 19;
10. 0.012; 11. 2.4; 12. 89

PAGE 84

1. 648; 2. 389; 3. 676; 4. 355;
5. 1,759; 6. 30.$\overline{66}$; 7. 58; 8. 116

PAGE 85 (DIAGNOSTIC TEST)

1. 2/3, 2. 1 5/72, 3. 1 5/24, 4. 1 1/48,
5. 41/60, 6. 7 7/20, 7. 7 8/15,
8. 8 1/2, 9. 9 1/12, 10. 4 14/15

PAGE 90

1. 1/3: 3, 6, 9, 12, 15; 2/5: 5, 10, 15,
20, 25; LCD = 15;
2. 1/2: 2, 4, 6, 8, 10; 3/4: 4, 8, 12,
16, 20; LCD = 4;
3. 5/6: 6, 12, 18, 24, 30; 2/7: 7, 14,
21, 28, 35; LCD = 42;
4. 1/4: 4, 8, 12, 16, 20; 4/5: 5, 10,
15, 20, 25; LCD = 20;
5. 1/3: 3, 6, 9, 12, 15; 1/4: 4, 8, 12,
16, 20; LCD = 12;
6. 2/3: 3, 6, 9, 12, 15; 3/8: 8, 16, 24,
32, 40; LCD = 24

PAGE 91

1. 1 1/3, 2. 13/18, 3. 1 2/3, 4. 17/18,
5. 1 5/12, 6. 1 1/10, 7. 1 3/10,
8. 1 1/14, 9. 1 1/21

PAGE 92

1. 1, 2. 1 1/6, 3. 1 5/14, 4. 1 4/15,
5. 1 4/9, 6. 1 3/10, 7. 3/8, 8. 1 1/8,
9. 1 7/12, 10. 1 1/3, 11. 1 3/8,
12. 1 2/5, 13. 7/9, 14. 5/6, 15. 1 3/14,
16. 1 3/8, 17. 5/6, 18. 1

PAGE 93

1. 7 1/6, 2. 8 1/10, 3. 9, 4. 9 5/6,
5. 9 5/14, 6. 7 7/10

PAGE 94

1. 9 1/2, 2. 12 5/6, 3. 5 9/10,
4. 7 4/21, 5. 8 1/12, 6. 9 1/3,
7. 11 4/9, 8. 6 19/21

PAGE 95

1. 9 2/9, 2. 8 5/8, 3. 11 1/6,
4. 12 1/6, 5. 5 14/15, 6. 8,
7. 8 3/14, 8. 8

PAGE 96 (DIAGNOSTIC TEST)

1. 17/24, 2. 7/12, 3. 3/10, 4. 1/4,
5. 9/20, 6. 2 3/14, 7. 4 7/10, 8. 3 3/4,
9. 2 1/18, 10. 2 1/14

PAGE 101

1. 1/12, 2. 1/10, 3. 13/45, 4. 1/6,
5. 1/6, 6. 5/8, 7. 1/2, 8. 1/3

PAGE 102

1. 1/2, 2. 7/15, 3. 1/10, 4. 5/12,
5. 1/10, 6. 17/24, 7. 2/9, 8. 3/14, 9. 0,
10. 11/18

PAGE 103

1. 17/24, 2. 1/4, 3. 53/90, 4. 3/14,
5. 11/21, 6. 7/12, 7. 7/15, 8. 1/6,
9. 3/14

PAGE 104

1. 2 9/8, 2. 3 7/4, 3. 4 5/4, 4. 1 11/6,
5. 1 5/3, 6. 3 6/5, 7. 14/8, 8. 2 9/5,
9. 3 15/8, 10. 5 3/2

PAGE 105

1. 11/14, 2. 2 5/6, 3. 1 17/18,
4. 3 5/8, 5. 1/2, 6. 2 3/8

PAGE 106

1. 1/6, 2. 4 1/2, 3. 3, 4. 1/6,
5. 5 11/14, 6. 1 5/8, 7. 3 5/14,
8. 2 3/4, 9. 3 2/3

PAGE 107 (DIAGNOSTIC TEST)

1. 3, 2. 9, 3. 6 2/3, 4. 32, 5. 2/9,
6. 1/2, 7. 3/20, 8. 16 1/24, 9. 21 3/8,
10. 2 2/3

CD-104227 • Jump Into Math • © Carson-Dellosa

ANSWER KEY

PAGE 112

1. 4, 2. 4 1/5, 3. 2, 4. 7 7/8, 5. 8,
6. 6/7, 7. 8/9, 8. 1 7/8, 9. 9/10,
10. 4 2/3

PAGE 113

1. three-fourths of 20, 15; 2. five-ninths of 9, 5; 3. one-fifth of 25, 5;
4. three-fourths of 100, 75;
5. seven-tenths of 100, 70;
6. two-fifths of 40, 16; 7. one-third of 18, 6

PAGE 114

1. 8, 2. 16, 3. 3, 4. 15, 5. 30, 6. 18,
7. 7, 8. 25, 9. 14, 10. 16

PAGE 115

1. 6/25, 2. 5/9, 3. 1/10, 4. 1/12,
5. 3/20, 6. 2/21, 7. 3/5, 8. 5/21,
9. 7/24, 10. 5/12, 11. 5/14, 12. 10/27

PAGE 116

1. 5/6, 2. 2/9, 3. 3/20, 4. 15/22,
5. 1/6, 6. 1/7, 7. 1, 8. 2/5, 9. 1/5,
10. 2/3

PAGE 117

1. 7 1/2, 2. 18, 3. 1/2, 4. 9 1/3,
5. 5/7, 6. 5/9, 7. 4/7, 8. 8, 9. 8/15,
10. 2/5

PAGE 118

1. 8 1/4, 2. 20 2/5, 3. 1 3/4,
4. 30 3/8, 5. 2, 6. 8 1/3, 7. 10 1/2,
8. 13 5/12

PAGE 119

1. 8, 2. 7 1/2, 3. 19 1/6, 4. 34 2/3,
5. 23 4/5, 6. 7 1/2, 7. 24 2/7,
8. 26 4/9

PAGE 120

1. 9 1/6, 2. 12 1/2, 3. 22, 4. 13 21/32,
5. 15 1/32, 6. 13 2/9, 7. 45,
8. 11 23/27, 9. 23 1/3, 10. 44

PAGE 121 (DIAGNOSTIC TEST)

1. 10, 2. 12, 3. 1/6, 4. 1 1/2, 5. 3/8,
6. 15/16, 7. 1/2, 8. 2, 9. 1 8/9,
10. 6 2/9

PAGE 125

1. 4/1 or 4, 2. 4/3, 3. 6/5, 4. 3/2,
5. 5/1 or 5, 6. 7/5, 7. 9/2, 8. 5/4, 9. 6,
10. 7/3, 11. 3, 12. 25, 13. 8,
14. 8 2/5, 15. 14, 16. 18, 17. 11 1/4,
18. 66, 19. 7

PAGE 126

1. 1/4, 2. 1/7, 3. 1/9, 4. 1/2, 5. 1/3,
6. 1/11, 7. 1/24, 8. 1/6, 9. 1/15,
10. 1/5, 11. 2/21, 12. 1/16, 13. 2/9,
14. 2/5, 15. 1/12, 16. 5/36, 17. 2/35,
18. 1/88, 19. 1/40

PAGE 127

1. 2, 2. 1/4, 3. 1/6, 4. 3/2, 5. 4/3,
6. 8, 7. 1/9, 8. 7/5, 9. 9/8, 10. 1/8,
11. 4 1/2, 12. 3/28, 13. 4 1/2,
14. 5/42, 15. 64, 16. 14 1/7, 17. 1/18,
18. 12 1/2, 19. 5/21

PAGE 128

1. 2 1/7, 2. 2/3, 3. 4/9, 4. 4/5,
5. 1 5/6, 6. 1/2, 7. 5/12, 8. 1/2,
9. 4/5, 10. 2/3

PAGE 129

1. 6 3/4, 2. 1 3/32, 3. 5/24, 4. 1 1/2,
5. 7/18, 6. 4/5, 7. 1, 8. 7/9, 9. 7/27,
10. 1 1/20

PAGE 130

1. 15/16, 2. 9/10, 3. 1, 4. 4, 5. 15/16,
6. 8/27, 7. 15/22, 8. 1 1/2, 9. 2,
10. 25/32

PAGE 131

1. 14/9, 2. 11/4, 3. 9/2, 4. 10/3,
5. 23/8, 6. 61/10, 7. 20/16, 8. 14/3,
9. 24/85, 10. 4 5/28, 11. 25/56,
12. 7 1/6, 13. 1 202/413, 14. 91/300,
15. 2 2/21, 16. 2 11/14, 17. 9/11,
18. 4 4/9

PAGE 132

1. E, 2. B, 3. H, 4. K, 5. A, 6. I, 7. C,
8. L, 9. D, 10. F, 11. G, 12. J

PAGE 133

Column A: 1. 1 1/3, 2. 10 2/3,
3. 7/96, 4. 25/56, 5. 6, 6. 24/35,
7. 33/52, 8. 1 3/7
Column B: 1. 1 4/5, 2. 1/2, 3. 3,
4. 77/264, 5. 4/5, 6. 11 1/4, 7. 3 3/57,
8. 6 3/4
Column C: 1. 14 1/7, 2. 1 57/68,
3. 2/5, 4. 1 1/2, 5. 1 1/8, 6. 8 17/18,
7. 1/9, 8. 21/68

PAGE 134 (DIAGNOSTIC TEST)

1. 5,445; 2. 366; 3. prime;
4. composite; 5. 3⁴; 6. 10 x 10 x 10;
7. 32; 8. 2 x 2 x 3 x 3; 9. 120;
10. 2 x 5 x 7

PAGE 142

1. 30, 54, 42; 2. 66, 36, 624, 8, 870;
3. 680, 2,360, 3,400, 4,568; 4. 33,
21, 9, 18; 5. 15, 45, 560, 50, 95,
3,405; 6. 120, 824, 768, 340, 116;
7. 455, 644, 161, 112; 8. 72, 324,
513, 90, 621

PAGE 143

1. Divisible by 2, 4, 8; 2. Divisible by
3, 6; 3. Divisible by 2, 4, 5, 8;
4. Divisible by 3, 9; 5. Divisible by
2, 4, 6; 6. Divisible by 2, 4, 8;
7. Divisible by 2, 3; 8. Divisible by 2;
9. Divisible by 2, 3, 6, 7

PAGE 144

1. Divisible by 2, 7, 8, 9; 2. Divisible
by 2, 3, 9; 3. Divisible by 3, 6, 7;
4. Divisible by 2, 3; 5. Divisible by 3;
6. Divisible by 2, 4, 8; 7. Divisible by
2, 3, 6; 8. Divisible by 3; 9. Divisible
by 2, 3, 6, 8

PAGE 145

1. Prime, 2. Composite, 3. Prime,
4. Composite, 5. Prime, 6. Prime,
7. Composite, 8. Composite,
9. Prime, 10. Composite,
11. Composite, 12. Prime,
13. Composite, 14. Composite,
15. Composite, 16. Prime,
17. Composite, 18. Composite

PAGE 146

1. Factors: 1, 3, 9, 27; Divisible by: 3, 9, 27; Composite; 2. Factors: 1, 3, 5, 15; Divisible by: 3, 5, 15; Composite; 3. Factors: 1, 17; Divisible by: 17; Prime; 4. Factors: 1, 19; Divisible by: 19; Prime; 5. Factors: 1, 2, 3, 6, 7, 14, 21, 42; Divisible by: 2, 3, 6, 7, 14, 21, 42; Composite; 6. Factors: 1, 31; Divisible by: 31; Prime; 7. Factors: 1, 2, 11, 22; Divisible by: 2, 11, 22; Composite; 8. Factors, 1, 41; Divisible by: 41; Prime; 9. Factors: 1, 37; Divisible by: 37; Prime; 10. Factors: 1, 5, 11, 55; Divisible by: 5, 11, 55; Composite

PAGE 147

1. 2^4; 2. 3^3; 3. 5^4; 4. 4^6; 5. 10^4; 6. 2^7; 7. 4^2; 8. 3^5; 9. 10^5; 10. 5^5; 11. 3 x 3 x 3; 12. 5 x 5; 13. 2 x 2 x 2 x 2 x 2; 14. 4 x 4 x 4 x 4 x 4 x 4; 15. 1, 16. 2 x 2 x 2 x 2 x 2 x 2; 17. 3 x 3 x 3 x 3; 18. 5 x 5 x 5 x 5 x 5; 19. 10 x 10 x 10, 20. 4; 21. 1,000; 22. 25; 23. 16; 24. 32; 25. 243; 26. 625

PAGE 148

1. False, 2. False, 3. True, 4. True, 5. True, 6. True, 7. True, 8. True, 9. True, 10. True, 11. False, 12. True, 13. True, 14. True, 15. False

PAGE 149

1. 2 x 2 x 2 x 3 x 5; 2. 2 x 2 x 2 x 3; 3. 2 x 2 x 3 x 3; 4. 2 x 2 x 3 x 5; 5. 3 x 3 x 5; 6. 2 x 2 x 2 x 3 x 3

PAGE 150

Check student's factor trees. Prime Factors: 1. 3 x 5; 2. 3 x 11; 3. 5 x 5; 4. 3 x 3 x 3; 5. 2 x 2 x 2 x 3; 6. 2 x 2 x 5 x 7; 7. 3 x 3 x 3 x 3; 8. 2 x 2 x 2 x 2 x 2 x 3; 9. 2 x 2 x 5

PAGE 151 (DIAGNOSTIC TEST)

1. –27; 2. –200; 3. 10; 4. –3; 5. –125; 6. <; 7. <; 8. <; 9. –5, –2, –1, 0, 6; 10. –8, –6, –4, –1, 0

PAGE 155

1. 5; 2. –15; 3. –12; 4. –27; 5. –8, 6. –30; 7. 25; 8. 45; 9. –8; 10. –7; 11. 6; 12. 800; 13. –1,000; 14. 124; 15. 8; 16. –7; 17. 50; 18. 45; 19. –185; 20. –15

PAGE 156

1. I, 2. M, 3. E, 4. K, 5. O, 6. B, 7. A, 8. G, 9. Q, 10. C, 11. S, 12. P, 13. D, 14. F, 15. H, 16. J, 17. T, 18. L, 19. R, 20. N

PAGE 157

1. 1, 2. 6, 3. –3, 4. 0, 5. –7, 6. 6, 7. –3, 8. 0, 9. 5, 10. –9, 11. 7, 12. –10, 13. 2, 14. –6, 15. 0, 16. –4, 17. 4, 18. 9, 19. –1, 20. –7

PAGE 158

1. –9, –5, 0, 1, 2; 2. –2, –1, 0, 1, 2; 3. –3, –1, 0, 1, 2; 4. –10, –6, –2, 4, 5; 5. –7, –6, –3, 4, 6; 6. –10, –8, –4, 1, 2; 7. –88, –2, 2, 8, 10; 8. –8, –4, 2, 6, 10; 9. –10, –4, –1, 2, 8; 10. –4, –3, –1, 2, 8

PAGE 159

1. –26, –14, –8, 4, 10, 22; 2. –10, –8, –6, 6, 16, 18; 3. –31, –17, 2, 5, 8, 34; 4. –14, –2, 2, 8, 9, 12; 5. –51, –48, –40, 5, 24, 44; 6. –36, –35, –17, 22, 25, 51; 7. –64, –48, –20, 21, 42, 72; 8. –79, –41, –31, 54, 57, 80; 9. –12, –11, –8, 8, 27; 10. –41, –31, –23, –21, 2, 40

PAGE 160

1. >, 2. >, 3. <, 4. <, 5. <, 6. >, 7. <, 8. <, 9. >, 10. <, 11. >, 12. <, 13. <, 14. >, 15. <, 16. >, 17. <, 18. >, 19. <, 20. <

PAGE 161 (DIAGNOSTIC TEST)

1. 21, 2. –59, 3. –10, 4. 3, 5. 0, 6. 5, 7. 28, 8. –3, 9. –20, 10. 14

PAGE 169

1. 7, 2. –6, 3. 4, 4. 7, 5. –5, 6. 2, 7. 10, 8. –9, 9. 2, 10. 2, 11. –6, 12. 6

PAGE 170

1. 10, 2. –6, 3. 4, 4. –10, 5. 2, 6. 9, 7. 9, 8. –7, 9. –4, 10. 0, 11. –1, 12. –2, 13. –8, 14. 8, 15. 1

PAGE 171

1. 10, 2. –10, 3. 2, 4. –15, 5. –10, 6. 0, 7. –10, 8. 10, 9. –9, 10. 16, 11. 4, 12. –12, 13. 15, 14. 2, 15. –4, 16. –1, 17. –3, 18. 1, 19. 2, 20. –2, 21. –3, 22. –3, 23. –10, 24. –10, 25. –5, 26. 1, 27. –1, 28. –8, 29. 8, 30. 2

PAGE 172

1. –5; 2. 6 + 4 = 10; 3. 4 + –5 = –1; 4. –5 + 4 = –1; 5. –6 + –6 = –12; 6. 8 + –4 = 4; 7. 7 + 4 = 11; 8. –9 + –5 = –14; 9. –3 + 6 = 3

PAGE 173

1. –3 + 2 = –1, 2. –3 + (–5) = –8, 3. –7 + (–2) = –9, 4. 10 + (–4) = 6, 5. 3 + (–7) = –4, 6. –5 + 12 = 7, 7. –9 + 9 = 0, 8. 5 + (–6) = –1, 9. –8 + 18 = 10, 10. –10 + 11 = 1

PAGE 174

1. 1, 2. 25, 3. –3, 4. 26, 5. –4, 6. 7, 7. –16, 8. –4, 9. 10, 10. –8, 11. -1, 12. –9, 13. 15, 14. -90

PAGE 175

1. 27, 2. 2, 3. 21, 4. –40, 5. 22, 6. –7, 7. –34, 8. 70, 9. 28, 10. 2, 11. –55, 12. -5, 13. 10, 14. –44, 15. 12, 16. 70

PAGE 176

1. 21, 2. –20, 3. –30, 4. 10, 5. 20, 6. –42, 7. 24, 8. –50, 9. 71, 10. –71, 11. 0, 12. 10, 13. –22, 14. 4, 15. 57, 16. 120, 17. 7, 18. –2, 19. –25, 20. –4, 21. –2, 22. –310

PAGE 177 (DIAGNOSTIC TEST)

1. 34%, 2. 87%, 3. 12%, 4. 20%, 5. 87.5%, 6. 47%, 7. 0.3%, 8. 1.8%, 9. 70%, 10. 125%

PAGE 181

1. 55%, 2. 20%, 3. 90%, 4. 40%,
5. 92%, 6. 34%, 7. 75%, 8. 80%,
9. 25%, 10. 70%, 11. 80%, 12. 40%,
13. 32%, 14. 20%, 15. 46%, 16. 85%

PAGE 182

1. 31.25%, 2. 37.5%, 3. 10%,
4. 80%, 5. 75%, 6. 25%, 7. 12%,
8. 87.5%, 9. 30%, 10. 43.75%,
11. 66.67%, 12. 8.$\overline{3}$%, 13. 83.$\overline{3}$%,
14. 50%, 15. 58.$\overline{3}$%, 16. 62.5%,
17. 33.$\overline{3}$%, 18. 83.$\overline{3}$%

PAGE 183

1. 35%, 2. 5%, 3. 77%, 4. 4%,
5. 134%, 6. 2%, 7. 16%, 8. 58%,
9. 8%, 10. 183%, 11. 43%, 12. 78%,
13. 109%, 14. 28%, 15. 6%,
16. 68%, 17. 156%, 18. 19%,
19. 1%, 20. 74%

PAGE 184

1. 0.60, 60%; 2. 0.625, 62.5%;
3. 0.29, 29%; 4. 0.08, 8%; 5. 0.50,
50%; 6. 0.75, 75%; 7. 0.6$\overline{6}$, 66.$\overline{6}$%;
8. 0.70, 70%; 9. 0.30, 30%;
10. 0.51, 51%

PAGE 185 (DIAGNOSTIC TEST)

1. 7.5, 2. 32, 3. 56.25, 4. 23.04,
5. 17.2, 6. 120, 7. 68.3%, 8. 55.24%,
9. 72.3%, 10. 50%

PAGE 190

1. 96, ?, 128; 2. 27, 90, ?; 3. ?, 12,
30; 4. ?, 125, 25; 5. 35, ?, 70;
6. 52.5, 150, ?; 7. 58, 105, ?; 8. 36, ?,
12; 9. 78, ?, 14; 10. ?, 50, 80;
10. 170.4, 240, ?

PAGE 191

1. 71.4, 2. 81.18, 3. 98.31, 4. 11.40,
5. 19.50, 6. 44, 7. 48, 8. 48,
9. 214.4, 10. 420

PAGE 192

1. 81, 2. 78, 3. 45.5, 4. 45, 5. 12,
6. 255, 7. 37, 8. 21, 9. 78, 10. 225,
11. 96, 12. 440, 13. 36.48, 14. 51.84,
15. 400, 16. 375

PAGE 193

1. $25.72, $43.78; 2. $33.50, $29.70;
3. $4.99, $14.96; 4. $8.99, $20.96;
5. $264.00, $536.00; 6. $10.80,
$79.19

PAGE 194

1. 50, 2. 75, 3. 160, 4. 100, 5. 560,
6. 300, 7. 600, 8. 500, 9. 600,
10. 185

PAGE 195

1. 445; 2. 557.14; 3. 226.67;
4. 2,000; 5. 400; 6. 937.5; 7. 437.5;
8. 180; 9. 275.76; 10. 500

PAGE 196

1. 30%, 2. 40%, 3. 80%, 4. 60%,
5. 35%, 6. 55.24%, 7. 30.75%,
8. 47.$\overline{7}$%, 9. 71%, 10. 37%

PAGE 197

1. 30%, 2. 29%, 3. 33%, 4. 40%,
5. 50%, 6. 20%, Laptop Computer,
Mountain Bike, Running Shoes,
DVD, Computer Game, Amusement
Park Ticket

END OF BOOK TEST, PAGES 198–201

1. A, 2. A, 3. D, 4. C, 5. B, 6. A,
7. C, 8. D, 9. B, 10. B, 11. C, 12. B,
13. B, 14. A, 15. C, 16. B, 17. B,
18. C, 19. B, 20. D, 21. B, 22. A,
23. C, 24. B, 25. C, 26. A, 27. C,
28. A, 29. D, 30. C

Certificate
OF COMPLETION

This is to certify that

_____

has completed the mathematics exercises in

Jump Into Math!

Grade 5

_____
SCHOOL

_____
TEACHER'S SIGNATURE

_____
DATE